Dignity
and
Respect

THE HISTORY OF LOCAL 831

Kevin Rice

UNIFORMED SANITATIONMEN'S ASSOCIATION,
LOCAL 831, I.B.T.

ISBN 978-0-615-31945-2

Printed in New York City by Oxford Lithograph .

Published by Uniformed Sanitationmen's Association,
Local 831, I.B.T.

Dignity
and
Respect

THE HISTORY OF LOCAL 831

Introduction

Since 1898 there have been over 100,000 municipal Sanitation Workers in New York City. During that same time period there have been 20 U.S. presidents, 23 governors, 20 mayors, and an uncounted number of Department of Sanitation commissioners – and in the last 50 years: one Union – Local 831.

This is its story.

It is a story about you and those before you. It is a heritage that should not and will not be forgotten. The struggles for decent wages and benefits are part of it, but it is importantly a struggle for dignity and respect for you and the work you do every day.

These words echo throughout the long history of this Union. It was the seeking of these goals that motivated all of its leaders. This was the reason for the strike of 1968. I will never forget the story I was told by the long time outstanding Union consultant Jack Bigel. John DeLury, Union President, in 1968 returned to a tense Union Hall after a meeting with the Mayor. The shop stewards had to decide the fate of this Union: give in to the Mayor or take a stand. Most shop stewards were young and the arguments raged. But finally an old time Italian shop steward stood up, and with tears streaming down his cheeks, said: "We may pick up garbage but from this day forward it will be clear that we can't be treated like garbage."

Why this book? It is to make sure that those in the future understand what it took to make the job what it is today. It is to recognize the great leadership this Union has been fortunate to have: DeLury, Ostrowski, Scarlatos, and Nespoli. It also details the significant contributions that others have made in service to the Union – Jack Bigel, Charles Moerdler, Jerry Klein, and Howard Rubenstein.

This book would not have been written without the help of many people, but two must be mentioned. One is the writer Kevin Rice, who spent countless hours interviewing, researching and writing this book. The other is the current President, Harry Nespoli: his untiring efforts to make this Union great and use its history to show the foundation, resulted in this publication.

In closing, I hope the readers of this book will appreciate what it took to get this Union to where it is now, and how unique and special this Union and its members are.

In solidarity,
Allen Brawer
Honored to be Consultant to Local 831

Acknowledgements

First and foremost, I would like to thank the rank and file, the brothers and sisters of the Uniformed Sanitationmen's Association, for having authored such an amazing history as theirs over the last fifty years. All that was necessary for me to do was research it and write it down, a task in which I was aided by many different business agents and shop stewards of Local 831. In addition, I am thankful for the countless hours that various other Union executives and principals were able to spend with me over the last few years. Their names include James Alongi, Michael Bove, Tony Casalaspro, Vincent Cassino, St. Joseph Middleton, James Parker, Nick Pisano, and former Local 831 Presidents Edward Ostrowski and Peter Scarlatos. And, of course, thanks to Harry Nespoli who felt compelled to get the Union's history down on paper, for new-hires as well as retirees. And it was Harry Nespoli who decided that the link between the 1968 sanitation strikes in New York City and in Memphis was so strong that it warranted taking a delegation from Local 831, myself included, to Memphis in order to further investigate the connection.

This book began, in many ways, sixteen years ago when I first met Jack Bigel at a conference dedicated to a discussion of the New York City Fiscal Crisis of the 1970s. I am extremely grateful to have had the opportunity to have met Jack, one of the lions of the New York City municipal labor movement. Even in his eighties, Jack's intellectual energy was unstoppable, and inspiring.

Also to be thanked are several of the professionals and consultants affiliated with Local 831, including labor lawyer Alan Klinger, without whose close reading and criticisms this book would have suffered. Likewise, I thank Burt Lazarin, senior partner of Policy Research Group, whose deep knowledge of the City and the Union have benefited this history greatly.

There was never a point in time when the presence of Allen Brawer and his ardent support for this project was not felt and appreciated. Allen, who is a founder and senior partner of Policy Research Group, worked for thirty years as an associate of Jack Bigel. After Jack Bigel's death in 2002, it was Allen Brawer who picked up the torch that continues to help light the way for Local 831.

Bernard DeLury, former U.S. Undersecretary of Labor and son of Local 831 Founder and President John DeLury, must be thanked for his help in filling in many gaps and for furnishing some of the archival material, especially that of the Association of Employees of the Incinerators.

At the beginning of this project I had a meeting for which I am still very grateful. It was with Joshua Freeman, Professor at Queens College, City University of New York, the dean of New York labor historians, who challenged me to explore more deeply the dynamics of Local 831 and to explain how this relatively small municipal union could have become so politically powerful.

I thank the National Italian American Foundation for their support for my research on the role of Italian immigrants in the labor movement among Street Cleaners.

Thanks also to the team of readers consisting of attorney Mel Wulf, educator Ellen Meyers, writer Seth Rolbein and unionist and Village person Anthony Nunziata.

The production of the book itself owes much to the skill of graphic designer Kristen vonHentschel, as well as to photographer Deirdre Portnoy who helped choose, assemble and organize the many photos and illustrations that add visual support to the story. Thanks also to Anna Duart for her organizational skills during the final stages of this book.

Finally, I thank my wife, Marla, for her infinite patience and belief in the value and importance of this project.

Contents

Chapter One

A Day in the Life of the Union Hall

"The 23.3 inches of snow which fell over 4 successive weekends in January meant inconvenience and delay for most New Yorkers. But for Sanitationmen, it meant a sharp rise in the number of injuries suffered on the job, and one death."
- USA President John DeLury on the toll that snow removal took in the winter of 1964-65, noting the death of 48-year old Sanman Frank Berlusconi who was fatally crushed when a drunken driver smashed into him while he was behind his truck.

It is still dark at 4:40 a.m. on the second Thursday of December as the headlights of a cream-colored car light the way into New York City. The driver of the car is Harry Nespoli. Nespoli, President of Teamsters' Local 831, also known as the Uniformed Sanitationmen's Association (USA), the Union that represents New York City's more than six-thousand Sanitation Workers.

It is a mid-December morning in 2007. As he turns onto the final leg to the Union Hall on Cliff Street just south of the Brooklyn Bridge, Nespoli listens anxiously to the weather forecast on the radio and probably glances up through the windshield at the starless sky above. Garbage collection – and the Union business that attends it – is the last thing on his mind at that moment. One thing, one event, one word – and all the Union business that attends *it* – has consumed him at that moment. Snow.

● ● ● ● ●

Snow turns Sanitation Workers into heroes in New York City. The men and women who remove garbage by day also clear snow by night. Likewise,

1

LOCAL 831 ARCHIVES

Sanitation trucks take on a snowstorm. The two trucks work in unison, as the second truck must pick up where the first left off, cutting a wider swath in the snow.

their 25-ton white sanitation trucks undergo a similar transformation. When snow arrives, huge yellow plows are attached to the same garbage collection trucks, turning them instantly into snow-clearing behemoths. The trucks, by dint of this changeover, perform two different jobs for the City. So do the Sanitation Workers. Men and women who collect the garbage on one shift, clear snow on the next. These Sanitation Workers must now navigate the plows through a giant urban obstacle course (and over treacherous objects like sewer covers). They lead the charge of "the snow battalions," column upon column of salt-spreaders, front-end loaders, and snow melting machines. It's the equivalent of an armored division of a modern army, soldiered in this case by Sanitation Workers.

Long Days, In and Out of the Union Hall

Doing battle with snow can mean double shifts, sometimes as long as 14 hours, and extended routes. It can add up to some hefty overtime pay. But it's also not that simple. Snow can mean problems for the workers that remove it. Judging by the non-stop ringing of the Union Hall telephones at the approach of a snowstorm, it means lots of problems.

Nick Pisano and Jim Parker are on the front line this morning. Both men are business agents – taking phone calls from members, shop stewards, business agents – anyone with a problem. It's busy every day when they start at 7:00 a.m., but on this Thursday morning, with a snow-storm threatening New York, their phones are ringing off the hook. They answer and speak fast, Pisano announcing his name before the Union's, while Parker cuts directly to "831" – the short version by which many Sanitation Workers identify their Union.

"Pisano, Local 831..."
"831, Parker..."

Pisano looks puzzled as he quizzes a Sanman on the phone.

Pisano: They're telling you what? They're switching day guys nights?

At the same time, Parker assures a Sanitation Worker that the Union will get through to Management, aka the Bosses, aka the Department, aka Worth Street.

Parker: What's it say on the board? No, they got it backwards...

The Department has given the word to every garage that San Workers who normally work days will swing to nights and night workers will switch to days. This will create havoc with the personal schedules of the workers. Men and women who, after their shift, are normally expected to go home and care for their children – because their spouses work – must now scramble to make sure that those children get sitters or day care. Vacations planned months earlier must get canceled. If a worker's spouse has a doctor's appointment and needs transportation, alternative arrangements must get made.

Parker: Your wife? She's going in for what... where? Talk to me.

If shifts do get jumped – "night guys days and day guys nights" is just one scenario – it can take days and sometimes weeks before all the workers get back to their normal schedules. The Union often prefers a different course of action, one that minimizes the disruption to the personal lives of its rank and file.

Pisano: That's what we're telling them... absorb the 12 to 8 into the 7...

There is a similar frenzy going on at 125 Worth Street. Preparations for a snowstorm will turn the Department of Sanitation's headquarters into its own sort of war room. Nothing is more important to the stature of the Department than its prowess in getting the snow off the streets of Gotham – and fast. Snow removal – or lack of it – is such a sensitive issue in New York that it has, in and of itself, often been made into a political football, a barometer of how well the current administration is doing overall.

This partly explains the Department's quickness to reallocate manpower without great consideration for the personal lives of workers affected by such decisions. This is actually just one more example of a classic situation that has taken place over the last two hundred years of labor vs. management. Management, whether confronted by an ordinary problem or catastrophic event or, in this case, potential snowfall, will often attempt to use Labor as an option to protect itself. Just as shock absorbers bear the brunt of potholes and bumps in the road, so has Labor been similarly used, to bear the first, and heaviest, brunt of the coming battle with snow. Sanitation Workers have, in this situation, often been treated no better than an automotive part, and just as expendable.

Union business agents, who form the next level up from shop stewards in the Union's chain of command, express it clearly in their own unique language:

Pisano: If he turns around and says no, watch out... Yeah... Harry talked to them. We got our own Plan B... and we got a Plan C. Sometimes they will just not accept a suggestion from the union that makes sense... They think they're gonna bounce us around like a Spaldeen.*

["*spaldeen*" is New York-ese for a rubber ball]

No one ever sits much on the second floor at Cliff Street – possibly a habit that veteran Sanmen picked up from years on a job that consists of constant motion – and by now Pisano and Parker are both on their feet, bouncing from call to call in what looks like a game of dueling telephones. The hustle and bustle of other business agents back and forth across a room half the size of a basketball court adds to the atmosphere of an athletic event. Jim Parker finishes up another phone call.

Parker: I hear what you're saying... instead of being a scumbag he's just being a prick... Okay... Done. You too. Have a safe day.

Parker ends many of his phone calls with "Have a safe day" or "Be safe out there." These words have special significance for men and women who have one of the most dangerous jobs in the United States today. Sanitation Workers suffer one of the highest rates of injury due to on-the-job accidents: constant cuts and lacerations from handling sharp objects, as well as accidents

LOCAL 831 ARCHIVES

A Christmas tree provides welcome added illumination as one Sanman directs his partner behind the wheel of a plow.

that can result in severed arms when a worker is snagged and sucked into the jaws of the truck's hopper. Another type of accident that occurs with high frequency is when a Sanitation Worker gets rammed by an oncoming vehicle and is crushed against the back of his or her truck. Also, what's hidden in the garbage may occasion injury. It might be vermin, resulting in a rat bite. But the worst scenario is when the garbage contains toxic or chemically volatile substances that explode in the face of a Sanitation Worker, resulting in blinding or disfigurement.

Those are just the accidents. Then there is the wear and tear that accumulates from the removal of millions of tons of garbage from the streets each year. It's a daily grind – week after week, month after month, year after year – of lifting, shifting, tugging, pulling, running, bobbing, weaving, and heaving. Collecting garbage in New York City requires Sanitation Workers to be a combination of professional athlete and contortionist.

Finally, figure in snow removal. Not just the double shifts and physical energy required to get rid of the stuff, but also the increased job hazards that result from snowy and icy conditions. From all of this emerges a rough picture of the physical toll the job of Sanitation Worker takes on the human body. That is why Parker's "Have a safe day" carries so much meaning. Sanitation Workers are sensitive to the issue of safety. Parker taps into this by poking fun at himself after putting the phone down for the umpteenth time, wagging his aching hand, and announcing to all around him: "I'm gonna get Carpal Tunnel today!"

The physical layout on the second floor of the USA Union Hall resembles that of a newspaper office. Its open design allows information to flow freely – this would not be an easy place to harbor secrets. Everything is out in the open – three rows of desks linked side to side, and then a separate row against the far wall – including Pisano's and Parker's – all with no enclosures around them. As in a news office, facts and phone calls must be dealt with instantly. When the phone rings, there is not a lot of chit-chat. Instead, everything is *now*. If a Sanitation Worker calls in with a problem before his or her shift begins, every attempt is made to deal with it before the shift begins. Incoming calls are treated like hot potatoes, questions and answers flying from business agent to business agent to Harry Nespoli himself, if necessary, until they are dealt with – usually in minutes, not hours.

Joe Middleton, a business agent from the Bronx, enters the room and flags down Nespoli. Middleton informs Nespoli that a steward in the West Bronx has some concern about a "new-hire" who will be going out to plow for the first time. Nespoli sums up the learning curve and the urgency to the job with the following comment: "He hits a raised sewer-cover, he'll learn fast enough."

The jumping of shifts that the Department is proposing will disturb the Union's regular system of communication. So will other logistical moves that the Department may make this morning. Snow imposes a different set of priorities than garbage collection. For example, because of their vital importance not just to the city's economy, but to the whole world's, Wall Street and the downtown Financial District are areas that get snow cleared first and fast. As a result, Sanitation Workers will get transferred to that district – and to many different districts away from their usual bases – as determined by the Department's snow removal strategy. In the meantime, however, shop stewards must remain at the garage. Their staying put is symbolic of the Union's presence and constant accessiblity. The redeployment of workers, however, will cut the stewards off from some or all of the workers who normally turn to them for problem-solving. This possible communication breakdown is what Nespoli wants to keep from happening.

Parker: Joe, I got Angie from Bronx Seven!

Joe Middleton takes the call. Middleton: "Yeah, sister, we're on the same page..." Middleton's voice trails off. About six-thousand of New York City's Sanitation Workers are men, and Middleton will call any one of them "Brother." By addressing one of 176 women on the force as "Sister,"

Middleton reflects the Union's perspective. Anyone within listening distance knows that brother and sister, in this Union's family, work in cooperation with each other to get the job done. As Middleton puts it, they are "on the same page." The battle with snow is confronted by men and women together, shoulder to shoulder.

And then it is over. Harry Nespoli hangs up the phone in his office, emerges and shouts to everybody in the room, "Okay, gang, listen up!" The business agents gather round in a huddle. Nespoli continues: "So they're gonna take the 12 to 8 and put them in the 7 to 4 for now – and that's it." This is no major victory for the Union – one shift of workers will be affected – but it is a small victory when the Department heeds the Union's input, and it is hundreds of such small victories – along with a few bigger ones – that Local 831 is built on. The Union advocated a more graduated and rational approach in preparing for the snowstorm, and the Department listened. Pisano's telephone manner lightens up.

Pisano: Yeah, we got the word... Somebody listened.

From the Department's point of view, the changes in staffing are always necessary in order to cope with the snow. From the Union's, they are only necessary when they are necessary.

The Union – like the Department – cannot stop the snow from falling. At the same time, the Union will – unlike the Department – make sure that the lives of Sanitation Workers are not thrown out of joint any more than necessary in fulfilling their responsibility for snow removal. That is what the tumult on the second floor of the Union Hall is about this Thursday morning.

● ● ● ● ●

Now, the storm before the storm ends, and the rest of the day begins.

Very few unions the size of the Uniformed Sanitationmen's Association have their own Union Hall in New York City. The importance of the four-story building at 25 Cliff Street consists of more than just its value as a physical asset. The Union Hall stands as a symbol of Union power and a haven to every Sanitation Worker, whether he or she has a simple question, a dire need, or just the impulse to stop in for a cup of coffee and bagel.

There was a time in the Union's history – in the mid-1960s – when Sanitation Workers were not always made to feel so welcome at Cliff Street. The old mentality of "You're lucky you've got a job" still pervaded the thinking of certain Union officials at that time. In fact, the Union Hall had an unlisted number in those days. Such is not the case today, as Local 831 prides itself on its openness and accessibility to Sanitation Workers around the clock. The business card that Harry Nespoli gives out to his Union's members lists not just his office phone, but his home phone as well. With that act, he is making a statement that reinforces the Union Hall's open-door policy.

For the remainder of this Thursday, with the storm approaching, Sanitation Workers come and go freely to the Union Hall. Two Sanmen who are working near the Union Hall come in during their lunch in order to get their Union cards renewed. Another Sanitation Worker, a veteran of 16 years on the force, has a question regarding her pension and is directed to the fourth floor. Next, the wife of a Sanman killed on duty shows up to inquire about the Union's death benefit. She is personally escorted to the fourth floor.

Michael Bove, the resident political strategist of Local 831 and a co-fighter of Union battles alongside Nespoli for over thirty years, has come down from his office on the fourth floor in order to review with his boss the Union's agenda for an upcoming meeting. In a few days Senator Hillary Clinton will come to Cliff Street and meet with Nespoli and his Executive Board, and then address the 300 men and women who are the Union's shop stewards.

Many political figures have made the rounds at Local 831 over the years in order to court the Union's favor. Just six weeks earlier, Mayor Bloomberg had also come, seeking support for his upcoming election. Clinton, however, will be only the second United States Senator ever to visit the Sanitationmen's Union Hall. The first was Robert Kennedy, who stopped by in March 1966 in order to personally apologize for a disparaging remark he had made about "garbagemen." Local 831 received him graciously and a grinning Kennedy danced his way out of the verbal misstep.

Nespoli, on his way out the door to a meeting of the Municipal Labor Committee, a coalition of the City's municipal workers, runs into Tony "Smash" Casalaspro who came on the job as a Sanitation Worker in the early 1950s. Nespoli tells Smash that the Union is planning to publish a book describing its history. Smash looks hard at Nespoli, then describes what it was like on the job more than a half-century ago.

It was tough, you know? Why, I remember after I went on the job and the first time I drove by my house. My mother and my sister were sitting on the stoop. So I beeped, you know... driving by in my truck I was proud so I laid on the horn with a couple of good beeps... but my mother and my sister turned their heads in the other direction... they wouldn't look at me. They didn't want to admit...

Smash chokes up for a moment, then grabs hold of himself and continues: "You see, back then... we were still called garbagemen. We didn't get no respect. Back in those days..."

And so Smash's history begins. It is the history of every Sanitation Worker and Street Cleaner, engaged forever in the struggle to improve their lives long before Local 831. The first president of the Union, John J.

Senator Hillary Clinton sits across from Harry Nespoli and other Union Executive Officers in the conference room of Local 831 Headquarters on Cliff Street in December 2007. At this meeting Nespoli expressed concern and consulted with Senator Clinton about matters – in particular, the Medicare Prescription Program – affecting Local 831 retirees.

DeLury, described that long-waged battle this way in 1965: "Our Union and its predecessors have a history going back to the 1890s... In this period we have slowly, painfully fought our way into the sun. And our Union – and other unions – will continue to fight when we have to fight."

This book is the story of the fight for dignity and respect that, in many ways, some old and some new, still goes on today.

In 1956, Local 831, as we now know it, was born. Its history begins with the story of how garbage was collected, and how the City grew, against the backdrop of the national labor movement and the immigrants of New York. It is there that we begin.

Chapter Two

Early Organizing

"Labor is prior to, and independent of, capital. Capital is only the fruit of labor, and could never have existed if labor had not first existed. Labor is superior to capital, and deserves much the higher consideration."
- Abraham Lincoln

"The contractors for cleaning the streets... do not anticipate any trouble in regard to obtaining laborers, not-withstanding the strike of the street sweepers."
- New York Times, July 2, 1865

"If a man is seen going up the City Hall steps with the look of a would-be suicide... ten to one he is a street cleaning contractor."
- Brooklyn Eagle, Sept. 3, 1869

The City's early attempts at providing sanitation services were abysmal failures.

And when it failed, the City often handed the job over to private contractors who performed even worse. The filth and refuse grew and, with it, public intolerance of the wretchedness. Citizens cried out for something to be done.

This desperate situation led to a singular action by City Hall. In 1872 street cleaning was placed under the direct supervision of the Police Department. It was not without historical precedent. The City had from its early history relied on police enforcement of street cleaning ordinances and sanitary regulations. Now, for the next ten years, the cleaning of the city's streets would fall squarely on the shoulders of the Police Department's new "Bureau of Street Cleaning." The police did not themselves perform the

This illustration is from 1868 and depicts street sweepers employed by private contractors as an unorganized bunch. What it does not show is the corruption for which those private contractors were known. Until the Department of Street Cleaning was finally formed in 1881, the City made many unsuccessful attempts to contract the job out.

work, but rather they attempted to supervise the casual labor force known as "Street Cleaners" or "sweepers."

In every precinct there is a patrolman who has special supervision of the work, his preliminary duty each day being the calling of the roll at 7am and the dismissal of the sweepers at 4pm.

This decade when police were put in charge of cleaning the streets resulted in spiraling budgets, scandal, corruption and anti-labor violence on a new scale. The Police Department appointed Captain Alexander "The Clubber" Williams, renowned for his brutality, to head up the street cleaning operations. When personnel and planning fell short, Williams and his thugs terrified and physically beat those Street Cleaners unfortunate enough to find themselves under his watch.

This period of police supervision of street cleaning lasted only ten years before the City, in 1881, mounted a major new effort at sanitation – and formed an entirely new entity, the Department of Street Cleaning, to administer it.

Uncontrolled Growth of the City

The police, in essence, threw back to the city a job they were no better equipped to handle than anyone else. The Herculean labor of cleaning the city was greatly compounded by rapid expansion of population, primarily from tens of thousands of newly arrived immigrants.

From 1800 to 1880, New York City's population roughly doubled every ten years. Gotham started the century with a little more than 30,000 inhabitants; eight decades later it was called home by more than a million people. By 1900, owing to its expansion and consolidation into five boroughs, the city counted 3 million residents inside its newly drawn borders. Waves of immigrants arriving from southern Europe and Russia in the 1880s soon made New York one of the world's largest cities. Primitive and sometimes non-existent sanitation ensured that it also became one of the dirtiest.

The contrast between a thriving city and its unsanitary conditions only reflected the starker contradiction between those who profited from its growth and those who paid for it with their working lives. Despite inventions like electricity and steam turbines, human sweat was still necessary for the wheels of business – and government – to turn. The surge in population, owing largely to immigration, provided the labor that made possible an unprecedented explosion in wealth. The treasure, however, was not shared equally. The filthy rich left the poor filthy. On the Lower East Side, working souls huddled together around pots of fish soup and potatoes in overcrowded tenements, while just a few blocks away on Wall Street, profits were piled high in the boardrooms of those who dined on foie gras at Delmonico's. Jacob Riis, a poor immigrant turned photojournalist, captured the situation in his master work, "How The Other Half Lives." Riis's photographs and writing put a focus on the squalid condition of the city's streets and the importance of street cleaning to the health and well-being of citizens.

The marriage of waste and wealth became a familiar feature on the emerging landscape of the Empire City. All the world's great urban centers – Rome, Paris, London – had at some point found it necessary to resolve the dilemma of refuse and riches. Never before, though, had the issue of sanitation grown to such nightmarish proportions so quickly as in New York of the mid-1800s. The solving of that problem would help determine just how great a city it was to become.

Garbage and gold always made uneasy partners, one resenting the other. The ancient confrontation between the two now became the setting for a meeting of new adversaries. It was no longer serfs fighting lords or peasants battling aristocrats. Now it was workers versus bosses. The second half of the nineteenth century marked the beginning of the struggle for unionism in the United States and, in the labor wars about to begin, New York would become a major battlefield. Among its early skirmishes were those between the men who cleaned the streets and those who acted as though they owned them.

Productivity and the "Power of Kings"

Riches and filth went hand-in-hand in the Industrial Age. "Dirty rich" and "filthy rich" described the wealthy in an era when profits – and garbage – spiraled to new heights. With the introduction of new inventions and energy sources, a new word, "productivity," rapidly found its way into the English language. But it was a concept that benefited, at first anyway, the bosses. The workers may have become vastly more productive during this period, but they continued to work 60-80 hour work weeks under often grueling conditions.

Labor had to play catch-up with management for the nearly the next fifty years. This was a period so turbulent that more than 36,000 strikes took place between 1865-1910. In fact, one of the first strikes of Street Cleaners in New York City took place in 1865, followed by dozens of small ones until the major Street Cleaners' Strike of 1907 erupted on the streets of the city.

Soon, labor leaders were also rolling around productivity in their mouths. Samuel Gompers, the "father of the U.S. labor movement" and first president of the American Federation of Labor, appeared before the U.S. Senate in August 1883 and several times referred to productivity as a means by which to shorten the work day to eight hours. Gompers emphasized that capital investments in machinery could both reduce the work day and result in an increase in production.

Gompers, who had started as an organizer among the cigar makers of the Lower East Side, was famous for the slogan, "A fair day's wage for a fair day's labor." His trade union movement adopted a basic live-and-let-live attitude toward management where he felt workers should stay out of the business of management – and politics – as part of the condition for any improvements they received. Unlike other more idealistic labor leaders, Gompers limited his efforts to improvements in pay, benefits and shortening the work day.

Gompers did not take any interest in organizing "unskilled labor," including the Street Cleaners of New York City. That mission fell instead to Terence V. Powderly, president of the Knights of Labor. Like Gompers, Powderly wanted to improve wages and benefits, as well as shorten the work day, but his organization had a bigger plan to create a whole new economic order that would "secure the toilers a proper share of the wealth they create." Powderly was a dreamer and, as such, he attracted some of the worst-treated groups of workers. It is no coincidence that among his followers stood a large contingent of New York City Street Cleaners.

Although slavery had supposedly been abolished two decades earlier, it simply put on a new face in the industrialism and westward expansion that lined the pockets of capitalists with gold. "We are slaves, if not in name, then in fact," bemoaned one worker.

The Street Cleaners of New York, in their first efforts to organize, often referred to themselves as "wage-slaves."

In New York City, Tammany Hall was king. Its rule of the city depended on and fed off the cheap labor of newly arrived hordes of immigrants. "Casual labor" became the norm, meaning that the City could hire people for pennies, and by the day. The only other courtesy that Tammany extended to workers consisted of giving them the power to vote, and the name to vote for, so that the bosses could stay in power.

Formation of the Department of Street Cleaning, 1881

In the Department's early years, the Tammany-connected Irish Americans had ruled and monopolized street cleaning jobs, both as sweeper and driver. Eventually the Italian immigrant started as laborer and, moving up the ladder, became a "brush man," or what was officially titled a "sweeper." The Irish were slower to let go of the job of driver, however, since it held greater status – and paid better. The occupation of driver implied strength: he sat high and controlled the movement of a powerful engine, the horse; he charted his own course and the speed at which to travel it. "Drivers" succeeded in keeping the title dominant over "sweepers" for the next fifty years, long after they had given up the reins for a steering wheel. The drivers in the department, also called "cartmen" or "teamsters" (if they had more than one horse), did not own their carts. Nonetheless, they tapped into the legacy of power that private cartmen had built up over the centuries. A "Drivers and Hostlers Union" first made known its demands in February 1882, less than one year after the formation of the new Department. They went on strike in an effort to get a pay increase and an end to work on Sundays and at night. It was an unsuccessful strike, with only limited worker involvement: "... fully half of the cartmen were ready to go to work, but were prevented from running more than one load of earth and garbage by the striking cartmen who, when the teams passed through ... stoned the drivers, and compelled them to leave their carts."

Despite the violence, the large numbers of readily available casual laborers doomed the strike to failure.

Street Cleaners First to Unionize

The first Labor Day Parade in New York City took place in 1882. But the labor movement had taken root in private industry and was still mainly confined to that realm. Organizing City employees was close to impossible in the 1880s. The public treated the City's workers as if they – especially the uniformed forces of police, fire and sanitation – were municipal property and had no rights as workers. When it came to the civil servant, the emphasis was on servant. One New York State Supreme Court justice summed up a commonly-held opinion at the time when he declared that "any combination of Civil Service employees as a labor organization or union is not only incompatible with the spirit of democracy but inconsistent with the spirit upon which our Government is founded."

Although true municipal unions were still decades away, there was one group of City workers that already seemed primed for organizing. As electric street lamps burned bright for the first time on Broadway in the early 1880s, the city's Street Cleaners were already carrying a different kind of torch directly into labor's battle.

The union movement that grew up among Street Cleaners, then, was a potent brew of occupational, ethnic and immigrant elements, all bubbling up in a time of great labor unrest. All it lacked was a catalyst to put it together. This need would soon be answered, strangely enough, with the appointment of one of the most colorful commissioners that New York City would ever see: Colonel George E. Waring.

Dashing Colonel Waring

Major scandals in city government coincided with the worst depression the United States had ever seen – the Panic of 1893 – and made possible the election of a reform mayor, William Strong, who wasted no time in trying to bring about change. His first candidate for Commissioner of Street Cleaning, Teddy Roosevelt, turned down the job in favor of becoming Police Commissioner. Roosevelt, with a reputation as a reformer, might have seen the challenge of the Police Department as the better springboard for his own political ambitions. In 1894 the Lexow Committee held hearings and took over 10,000 pages of testimony that exposed corruption on a scale that shocked even New Yorkers. The police were found guilty of pulling the strings and reaping profits from every center of criminal activity at the time: brothels, gambling, confidence schemes, shakedowns, election-rigging, and even abortions. The only place more dirt could be found than in the Police Department was on the streets of New York, the result of the lightweight and inept administration of Street Cleaning Commissioner Andrews.

Taking a broom to the mess that existed inside the Department of Street Cleaning in 1895, not to mention the one piling up outside on 420 miles of Manhattan streets, was a job for either a god or a madman. Mayor Strong's second choice for the job, Colonel George E. Waring, seemed a little of both.

Waring was a unique blend of urban and rural man. A decorated Civil War veteran who preferred his old title of "Colonel" to that of Commissioner, he had started his career in the field of agriculture. He came to specialize in drainage and from there proceeded to become one of the world's leading experts on sanitation. His foremost credit lay in his successful design of a modern sewage system in Memphis, Tennessee. From then on his services were widely sought throughout the country and although it was said that he had better-paying offers at the time, he welcomed the challenge of cleaning up America's greatest metropolis.

The first Street Cleaners Parade in 1896, as "White Wings" march in precision down Fifth Avenue. The parade was considered a success for the new Commissioner, Colonel George Waring. The men, however, griped at being forced to attend parade rehearsal before their morning shifts – and for no pay.

Photos often show the Colonel on horseback, as if he just rode in from a battle in the Civil War. In an odd way, his old-fashioned approach and largely self-created image of romantic hero made him a fitting candidate for the job, since municipal housekeeping in New York was still mired in the ancient past.

As late as the 1850s, pigs and goats, and dogs and cats roamed freely and scavenged kitchen scraps left out for them. Children played among piles of refuse and on the streets in what little room was left from the thousands of carts parked every which-way at night. People littered without a thought and thousands of empty lots turned into makeshift dumps. Motor cars were then only starting to appear; the horse still held sway. What it also held, and released daily, was about twenty-five pounds of manure. A count of more than 150,000 horses in the city at that time thus deposited three million pounds and more of the stuff on the streets every day. Cobblestone streets were still the rule (asphalt-paving was only just beginning by the 1890s) and, despite the best efforts of Street Cleaners to scrape them up, animal droppings clung tenaciously to the large spaces between the stones. To complete the picture, one must also add the drippings of body fluids and blood that flowed freely from the city's hundreds of slaughterhouses located on both the West and the East side. Some of this effluent eventually found its way into the Hudson and East rivers; the rest trickled into the streets. In addition, tens of thousands of animals dropped dead on the streets every year (15,000 horses in 1880 alone), their carcasses left to rot until they were hauled away.

Even in the "nicer" sections of the city, it was common practice to toss garbage and excrement directly onto the street below. Ladies wore parasols to protect themselves from such unwelcome missiles and gentlemen provided further tactical support by flanking them on the outside of the sidewalk. Refined members of both sexes sprinkled cologne on their handkerchiefs to mitigate the stench. Boots and a newer form of footware – rubbers – became required apparel for walking on the streets.

Collection of household refuse was irregular and infrequent, with rubbish in many places rising to a height of several feet. Once carted away, most was loaded onto scows which were then towed up by tugboats for dumping in the ocean. But often, as soon as they were out of sight – or "just out of gunshot range," as one scowman later testified – garbage scows would drop their loads in shallower water. In the decade before Waring took over, more than a million cartloads of trash were getting dumped each year into the not-so-deep blue and quickly finding its way back onto local beaches.

White Wings a.k.a. Waring's Color Scheme

One of Waring's most daring actions was to change the color of Street Cleaners' uniforms to pure white. The public and the press, at first, thought the move crazy. But as his men were about to find out, if Colonel Waring was crazy, he was crazy like a fox.

In the three short years he served as commissioner, Waring dazzled skeptics by making the Street Cleaning Department a model of efficiency and the pride of the city. He announced with ceremony the transformation of rag-tag band of Street Cleaners into a quasi-military force. He even proposed – to the disbelief of many – a Street Cleaners' parade down Fifth Avenue. At the dawn of the twentieth century, it looked as though the sun would once again shine on the streets of New York. The public embraced the new Commissioner as their darling. However, he got a somewhat rougher reception at the hands of Street Cleaners.

Waring's Labor Troubles

The strongest initial opposition to Colonel Waring came from the young labor movement among Street Cleaners. The Commissioner who could do no wrong from the public's perspective could do almost no right when it came to dealing with the men who worked for him. Although Colonel Waring talked

MCCLURE'S MAGAZINE, SPECIAL COLLECTIONS DIVISION, UNIVERSITY OF WASHINGTON LIBRARIES

Lone Street Cleaner (White Wing) attending to business. The brush, cart and water can were the essential tools and emblems of the City's Street Cleaners. Miles walked on foot, not to mention the cracks between the cobblestones, made the job particularly difficult.

about the dignity of his work force and the nobleness of their "fighting daily battles with dirt," it turned out that the fiercest daily battles his men fought were with their new boss.

Less than a month after taking over, Colonel Waring was confronted by the Drivers and Hostlers Union of the Department. Michael Kennedy, chairman of the union's executive board, stated their demands: that there be extra compensation for working on Sunday, that a driver not showing up for work on Saturday not get docked for two days (loss of Saturday and Sunday pay was the normal penalty imposed by the Department), that an end be put to the practice of Department superiors demanding blackmail, that an end also be put to the placing of Department "spies" among the men, and that the men be notified of the "entering of the next judgment" for an increase in wages. Kennedy, representing the Irish American contingent inside the Department, also criticized the Department for its continuing use of Italian immigrants.

Waring's response was that of a man spoiling for a fight. He stated, for example, that he would not only continue, but planned to expand the Department's policy of using spies to keep an eye on its work force. And although he gave a date as to when he would consider an increase in wages, he offered little hope of one, pointing out that he could hire men for $1.50 a day instead of the $2.00 a day ($60 a month) that drivers then earned. The Colonel, in fact, announced his intention to roll back wages:

I can get men... who would be only too glad to get a life position with a fair prospect for a pension in old age, with steady work and assured pay, for $45 per month. In my judgment, the old wages of $50 per month was not only ample, but under all circumstances, bountiful.

Waring then cut wages to $50 a month ($600 a year), a drastic 17% cut that ensured him even of more troubles to come with his workforce. In his response, the Colonel makes mention of the "prospect for a pension." Despite their desire to get a pension, Street Cleaners did not have one at this time. Waring's remarks began a tradition of empty pension promises that Street Cleaners would continue to have dangled in front of them for the next twenty years.

Colonel Waring got himself in deeper when, the following week, he attacked the labor union, calling it an "aristocracy." He also at that time indicated that he would continue the Department's policy of hiring "extras," a practice which had long been unpopular among his regular force. "Extra" was the term used for temporary workers who served as day laborers for the Department. At a time when there were no motorized plows, a major snowstorm could produce an instant need for as many as 20,000 snow shovelers for a day or a week. This had been made abundantly clear in the Great Blizzard of 1888, a weather event that further underscored the City's deficiency in clearing the streets of snow – and garbage. Eventually, other jobs (dump picker, scowman, scow trimmer and others) were filled by these temporary workers as the Department expanded the function of extras to suit its needs.

Women to the Rescue – Led by the Extraordinary Josephine Shaw Lowell

It took the "women's movement" to focus public attention on the city's Street Cleaners. Made up of mostly upper-class women, their embrace of

LOCAL 831 ARCHIVES

Casual laborers shoveling snow in Longacre Square (now Times Square) after the Great Blizzard of 1888. The ferocious storm shut down the city's transportation and made clear the need for a subway system. The poor performance by the Department of Street Cleaning in the wake of the storm also underlined the shortcomings of its dependence on casual labor to handle snow removal.

political and moral reform led them quickly to the cause of labor. At first, they addressed child labor and the welfare of working women. However, their strong interest in sanitary reform soon acquainted them with street cleaning operations and the labor problems that beset it. For many, it appeared to to view "municipal housekeeping" as an extension of their domestic roles. They considered the city their house, and the streets "the hallway."

These women helped Colonel Waring find a more conciliatory approach to his "labor problems." The Women's Municipal League, a powerful agent of progressive change at the time, conducted regular inspections of the streets and the Department's stables. The League even proposed that women get appointed as the official street inspectors. What had started as a "domestic" interest soon turned political. And, in the process, their desire to improve the conditions of the streets soon evolved into a desire to improve the conditions – and the pay – of the men who cleaned those streets. Before long the Women's Municipal League had become the champions of the White Wings.

No woman put her mark on the early Street Cleaners' labor movement

21

more than the founder of the Women's Municipal League, Josephine Shaw Lowell. As a leader of the women's movement, Lowell soon became a fierce advocate for better working conditions – especially for shorter hours – for the city's workers, including Street Cleaners. She recognized the right of workers to organize and called on other women to help "found trade organizations where they do not exist and assist existing labor organizations to the end of increasing wages and shortening hours."

Lowell corresponded with Colonel Waring when he was first beset by labor troubles. It was she who, in a series of letters to Waring, recommended the setting up of a "Board of Conciliation" to deal with the Street Cleaners' grievances and demands. Her influence was at least partly responsible for Waring's setting up a grievance apparatus, the "Committee of Forty-One," to settle those matters. As Lowell wrote:

> I believe in the right to strike; but remember that a strike is like war; it brings great misery with it... What I want to do, is, with others, to prevent strikes...

> When labor organizations and organizations of employers act together in joint boards of conciliation, they are, of course, far more effective for this purpose than when the two bodies act alone and often in opposition to each other.

> If by means of such organizations the relations between employers and employed could be adapted on an enduring and satisfactory basis, all causes of strife and contention removed... wages increased... strikes and turnouts prevented... the health and comfort of the workmen looked after, and other matters discussed and regulated, who would say that such results would not be worth any sacrifice that they might cost?

With labor harnessed to a degree, and with growing public support, Waring was able to modernize garbage collection, and institute an even more radical concept for the time: recycling.

Productivity Finds Its Way Into The Department

Once firmly at the reins, Colonel Waring organized and systematized the city's handling and disposal of waste. His new system required residents to sort refuse into three categories: ash, garbage (food and vegetable matter, also called "swill") and rubbish, consisting of all other refuse. Three different cans were placed outside residences. There was nothing revolutionary about this system (Boston had been separating its refuse in that manner for over a decade) except that it had never been done before in New York City. Not only did Waring's force clean the streets, they cleared them as well. Sixty-thousand carts were no longer allowed to stand vacant on the street overnight. Regulations were strongly enforced.

Waring also mustered strong public support for these initiatives. His own best salesman, he made frequent appearances before citizens groups. He oversaw the founding of the Juvenile Cleaners' League which recruited thousands of New York City schoolchildren to help monitor the condition of the streets and discourage littering. Waring intended for this youth to form the vanguard of a new consciousness toward waste and sanitation.

It was Waring's hope that the city – and not just private scavengers and scow trimmers – should reap value from its waste. If refuse were to be burned, Waring argued, then incinerators should be designed to generate electricity. As one observer put it, Colonel Waring wanted to use waste to "light the city."

Waring's timing was perfect. All the ingredients for change – Sanitary Reform, Tenement Reform, and a total rehabilitation of the Police Department – came together in early 1895 and provided critical support for the Colonel's new programs.

Sweeping changes in the civil service also increased Waring's odds for success. The City created a Labor Bureau in order to oversee civil service reform and hiring. Most importantly for Waring, the civil service was for the first time extended to cover laborers in public works, including street cleaning. Prior to that, graft was the key to getting a job and the typical Tammany street cleaner was hired only after campaigning for a ward boss or party chieftain, or making a payoff to one of their underlings. As reported in the New York Times of May 2, 1895:

> **In extending the civil service so as to apply to such laborers, the district leaders and politicians have been deprived of the patronage with which they have heretofore built up their power and influence. It will in future only be necessary for a person wishing employment on public works to go directly to the Labor Clerk, file an application, pass a physical examination, and await appointment.**

The new Labor Bureau, located in a small room in the Criminal Courts Building on Centre Street, was not ready for the crush of sixteen hundred men that came to apply for jobs on its first day in business. Only fifty men were let in at a time by the Labor Clerk E. P. Cringle who, interestingly, had been previously employed in the Street Cleaning Department and who recognized many of the applicants that morning as men who had "tried often to get employment in the Street-cleaning Department, but have been rejected for one reason or another."

One of the applicants looking for work on opening day declared:

The politicians are no longer in it. We can come here and get our positions directly and without having to curry favor with the district leaders. It gives every man a fair show. The poor man will have a chance now to get work without joining a political club or organization.

Colonel Waring seized this opportunity to overhaul his whole force. He had accepted the job from Mayor Strong on the condition that he would have total control over the Department, including hiring. The new civil service regulations gave him the tool to carry out his internal housecleaning and get rid of the Tammany-appointed deadwood. As Waring described it, he "put a man instead of a voter behind every broom."

From White Angels to White Wings

One of Waring's most daring decisions resulted in a radical change of uniforms for the force. As of July, 1895, every street sweeper was forced to buy white pants, white shirt and white pith helmet. It was an outfit more suited for safari than street cleaning, and the men immediately became the objects of ridicule.

Waring's supporters first tried to dub the Street Cleaners "White Angels," a strained attempt to link the men with a boss who had been dubbed "The Apostle of Cleanliness." His was a title less ironic than it might seem, since it was bestowed on Waring at a time when it was firmly believed that "cleanliness is next to godliness." Most citizens, however, resorted to calling the newly-clad workers "White Wings," since these new uniforms were made from duck cloth, commonly called "white duck." The name had other meanings as well. "White Wings" was a poetic way of referring to the sails of a boat, or to an angel, and it was also New Yorkese for fried eggs. "White Wings, sunny side up," or "Poached White Wings," were standard items on any downtown breakfast menu in the 1890s. The name was meant as a joke.

Waring cared less what his sweepers were called than that they were seen. Although some of his true faithful rationalized the white uniforms as Waring's attempt to have Street Cleaners dressed in a color associated with the medical profession, this was not true. For the same reason that the Police Department forced cops to start wearing blue in 1852, Waring dressed Street Cleaners in white in 1895 – so that the bosses could keep an eye on the workers. As Waring himself stated to the press:

A distinguishing and conspicuous uniform is necessary to keep some of the members of the force at their work... I think it would be safe to offer a large reward to any man in New York who will find one sweeper playing cards or otherwise idling

away his time, in a liquor saloon or elsewhere, while he is in his white uniform.

Once again, as with its policy of employing spies, the Department demonstrated a deep distrust of its workforce. The uniforms remained unpopular with the men for as long as they had to wear them and with their wives for as long as they had to clean them.

With time, uniforms helped establish a unique identity for what would come to be called the city's "essential forces" – police, fire and sanitation. But to the Street Cleaners of 1895 in their virgin white get-up, it was clear from the start that they would have to work harder than ever.

"The Committee of 41"
A Labor-Management Tool Ahead of its Time

With labor nipping at his heels and at the urging of labor advocates like Josephine Shaw Lowell, Colonel Waring adopted what was for its time a radical approach: he instituted in February 1896, the beginning of his second year at the reins, a regular labor management meeting called the "Committee of 41." The hope was to find a "method of treating possible causes of serious difference between the men and those in authority over them." The immediate aim was to deal with the hundreds of unaddressed grievances that the men brought up against the Department each year. Waring's larger goal was to defuse the constant threat of strikes.

The structure was simple: representing the sweepers and drivers were 32 men chosen from Section Stations and 9 from Stables. They formed a General Committee which elected 5 Spokesmen who then represented the entire workforce. The General Committee met three Thursday afternoons a month at 2:00 p.m. and did not have their pay docked for this time. At these meetings they discussed their grievances, questions concerning pay and other matters in secret. They then decided what they wished to bring up before a monthly "Board of Conference" where they met with the Commissioner and representatives of the Department.

The Board of Conference held its first meeting on February 20, 1896. The men were skeptical at first and clearly distrusted their boss. As Waring put it:

They were warned... to "look out for Waring; this is one of his tricks." That any Commissioner of Street Cleaning, even though he were an "angel," should honestly intend... to deal fairly with the rank and file of those under him, was too much to believe. There must be, they thought, some sinister motive behind it."

With time, the two sides came to trust each other and work together effectively. Waring wrote of these meetings and the respect he developed for the five Street Cleaners' Spokesmen:

Special mention must be made of the character and intelligence of the five members chosen to represent the men on the "Board of Conference." Uniform courtesy, gentlemanly, but firm adherence to parliamentary rules, and a thoroughly impartial performance of the duties of a Chairman characterized them.

During its first year of operation, the "Committee of 41" considered 345 cases. A total of 221 were settled by the Street Cleaners among themselves, and 124 were referred to the Board of Conference.

The men's grievances sprang from unfair or cruel treatment at the hands of foremen; late pay; forced work on Sundays: and docking of pay for no good reason. From its side, the Department sought action against men that it found guilty of any one of fifty offenses, including the following: absence from roll call; deliberately trotting or galloping a horse; loitering at work; and neglecting to pick up small stones found on route and failing to report large ones or other obstructions to section foremen.

Waring, by his own admission, reaped an unexpected benefit from the new setup: suggestions and input by the Street Cleaners as to how to get the job done more efficiently. This became one of the first exercises in labor and management consulting jointly on how to operate the department efficiently – a forerunner of the modern productivity program that would come into effect nearly a century later.

Together, the Department and the men who labored under it achieved something the city had not seen in seventy-five years: clean streets. The other problems that Waring did not get around to tackling – the ultimate disposition of waste, the recapturing of value from garbage either through its sale to private contractors or by burning it to run generators, and the growing menace of industrial pollution – these were forgiven the man who brought clean streets back to the city.

Mayor Strong also helped out by backing Waring's $3,300,000 budget request for the Department – a whopping 7 ½ % of the city's total budget of $42 million at the time. With this kind of funding and a force of 2,500 Street Cleaners, the Colonel was in a good starting position to get the job done. It should also be noted that Waring's New York City consisted only of Manhattan and its 420 miles of streets. Brooklyn, with 454 miles of streets, was not yet a part of New York City and would not be until after Waring's time. Brooklyn, like Queens, had its own separate Street Cleaning Department.

Colonel Waring was already being hailed a hero by the public when, in the spring of 1896, he organized the first Street Cleaners' parade that the city had seen. At first, there was jeering, then the jeers became cheers of crowds shouting their admiration for the military precision that Waring had forced upon ranks of parading White Wings. His own men, however, still did not trust him. The parade itself reflected one of the roots of their mixed feelings. The men, many against their will, had been forced to rehearse the march for weeks, and for no pay, before the 6:30 a.m. roll call.

Jacob Riis wrote that "it was Colonel Waring's broom that first let light into the slum." True though that may have been at the time, it was a light that shone briefly. Three short years later, Tammany swept the next elections, Waring was out, and filth was back. Most of the Colonel's reforms, including his ambitious program of recycling, were discontinued or lost in a return to business as usual, that is to say, rampant graft and corruption.

The Colonel rose with meteoric speed and, in the end, he did not so much fade as fizzle, a shooting star to New Yorkers wishing for a cleaner city. His lasting legacy would appear to have been the new white uniforms of Street Cleaners, but even those, within a few years, were discarded in favor of new colors.

Chapter Three

The Italians Have Arrived

"They say you are free in this great and wonderful country. I say that politically you are... but I say you cannot be half free and half slave, and economically all the working class in the United States are as much slaves now as negroes were forty and fifty years ago."
- Arturo Giovanitti, union organizer

Immigration from Italy increased dramatically after 1880. Newly arrived Italian immigrants started at the bottom, taking the most dangerous and dirty jobs such as laborers and longshoremen. By the 1890s, more than 90% of the public works laborers in New York City were of Italian extraction.

Many became Street Cleaners, scow men and dump laborers in the Department of Street Cleaning. The work was backbreaking, but the Italians, mainly young men from southern Italy, were of sturdy peasant stock and no strangers to hard physical labor. They worked 10 hours a day, six days a week for a dollar a day.

On A Scow and A Prayer

There was no more dangerous a job than working on the floating deathtraps known as scows. Scowman was a position filled almost exclusively by Italian immigrants. A scow was a low raft-like work boat on which the Department would pile up to 500 tons of garbage that was then towed out by a tug and dumped at sea. The Italian scowmen regularly risked their lives on these less-than-seaworthy vessels. Loading was the easy part. Dumping was a different matter. The off-loading was done by a crew of ten to twenty scowmen who, once they had voyaged the required distance out to sea (or out

SPECIAL COLLECTIONS, UNIVERSITY OF WASHINGTON LIBRARIES

Crews of about twenty Italian laborers, employees of the Department of Street Cleaning, trying to maintain their footing as they use pitchforks to shovel off a mountain of garbage into the sea. The practice was stopped during the reign of Colonel Waring, but resumed again in 1900 and continued until 1934. Garbage washed up from New Jersey to Connecticut. The work was dangerous under the best of conditions. Scows frequently broke loose of the tugs and then remained adrift in the open sea. Their crews of laborers, with no protection from the elements, sometimes drifted for days before they were rescued by other ships or floated back to shore on their own. Many were never seen again.

of eyesight from land), then used pitchforks to shovel off their load into the waters below. Sailing atop a mountain of garbage was perilous at all times, but especially in the heavier and often stormy seas of late fall and winter.

Worse still, the scows, with no means of power or navigation, frequently broke away from the tugs and drifted out to sea with their crew aboard. Days or weeks later, rescues of scows took place as far away as eastern Connecticut, Rhode Island and New Jersey. Some scowmen were not so lucky. Their scows sank or drifted off, lost at sea and the laborers were presumed dead.

The following excerpt from the Times in April 1879 described the hazardous conditions aboard a scow:

The scows are all nearly rotten from age and nearly dismantled from hard usage and are absolutely unseaworthy. Since

Labor unrest and the threat of strikes were boiling up frequently at the turn of the century. The pay of $2 a day might not have been so bad if it was given in return for what was supposed to be an 8-hour day. Instead, Streetcleaners were forced to work 10-12 hours a day, six days a week, with no overtime. The strikes continued to grow in intensity until the explosive Street Cleaners' Strike of 1907.

BROOKLYN EAGLE,
JANUARY 8, 1900

NUARY 8, 1900.

STREET CLEANERS COMPLAINING.

They Lay Charges Against McCartney Before the District Attorney.

Formal charges have been presented to the District Attorney against Street Cleaning Commissioner James McCartney by members of his department. It is claimed that the eight hour law has been constantly violated, the men declaring that they are made to work ten and twelve hours a day.

The names of a number of witnesses, as well as those men who make affidavits are in the hands of Assistant District Attorney McIntyre, who, in the absence of District Attorney Gardiner, received the charges. Accompanying the charges is the request that the attention of the Grand Jury be brought to the matter and that it investigate it.

At a meeting of the Street Cleaners' Union, held yesterday at 312 East Forty-seventh street, Manhattan, a committee was appointed to call on Mayor Van Wyck and other city officials, who, they believe, ought to know the conditions under which the men are working, and inform them of some of their grievances.

These men claim that the water-proof uniform they are wearing costs them $2.50, and they declare it is not worth more than $1.50. The hats they are wearing they claim cost them $1.50, while they are not worth, it is said, 75 cents, and can be purchased in only one place. A strike is threatened.

Saturday last the prevailing easterly winds have kept them from going out into the Lower Bay. Last Saturday eight scows, loaded to an extent which nearly admitted the water over their scuppers were sent out in tow of one of the regular tugs. They were manned by 150 Italians and scarcely had the uncouth fleet got beyond the Narrows when the heavy sea caused the old scows to roll and pitch in an alarming degree, prostrating the wretched Italians with sea-sickness. Several of the stout hawsers parting four of the scows went adrift. One of them was carried by the tide in the direction of the Romer Rocks, upon which she would have been wrecked a few minutes after had not a tug gone to her assistance. At midnight the scows returned to the City as heavily laden as when they started...

Capt. Gunner expressed the opinion that it was an outrage to oblige the department to send the Italians to sea in such manifestly unsafe vessels as those now at his disposal.

Many of the Italians worked 8-9 winter months and then went back to Italy for the summer months. These "birds of passage," as they were called, helped keep the Department of Street Cleaning supplied with the thousands of "extras" on which it increasingly relied in order to fill the less desirable jobs and to deal with snow removal. They were recruited from the large pool of immigrants in New York and sometimes even brought in from neighboring cities like Philadelphia.

The budding union movement among Street Cleaners considered the hiring of extras "obnoxious." This attitude was partly fueled by the fact that many of those early organizers were Irish-Americans who resented the upstart Italians. But the Department found extras extremely desirable. The transient status of the Italians made them relatively disposable, easily replaceable, less able to organize, and thus attractive to management. Some of the bosses also had a financial motivation to hire extras, as it was common practice to demand as much as a month's wages in advance from prospective job applicants.

The Padrones

Those were not the only shakedowns. In the 1880s and 1890s, extras were mainly recruited through the services of "padrones" who provided contracted Italian immigrants in return for a payoff up front. This system of payoffs for jobs paralleled that of Irish-dominated Tammany. One Victor Corbo, representing the Italians in the Department, hired a lawyer and went to City Hall to protest their having to "buy" their jobs: "All the men have to pay. All the Italians who want to work must pay, some as high as $35 or $50."

Italian immigrants at that time – whether they were transient workers or had come to stay – did not have the political tradition of previous immigrant groups like the English, Irish or Germans. Italy had until recently been a very fragmented collection of states and only in 1861 did it organize a centralized government and begin its modern history as a self-standing country. These immigrants from Italy were divided by dialect, by relations, by culture and cuisine, into groups of different regions. One observer at the time wrote: "They became Americans before they were ever Italians." Because of their great presence in the Department, one might also say that they became Street Cleaners before they were ever Americans.

The solidarity of culture that developed among Italian Street Cleaners owed to more than just the job they had in common. They were also subjected as a group to taunting ethnic hatred in the form of derogatory names directed toward them. "Dago" was just one term used to describe the Italian immigrant. Interestingly, it is a word that is thought to come from a phrase applied to casual laborers: "Work a day, then go." Another slur, "Guinea," carried racial overtones. In fact, immigration authorities recorded Italians as "non-whites" when they disembarked in New York. "Wop" also became a term used to derogate Italians and Italian-Americans.

Because transient workers were less likely to be committed to unions or simply because they were desperate to do the bidding of the padrones for a few dollars, Italian immigrants were sometimes exploited as strike breakers. And so it was for many reasons that the Italians became targets of prejudice and hatred, sometimes verbal and sometimes violent. Being a threat to the Irish inside the Department was alone enough of a liability to ensure rough treatment. But the occasional turns some of them took as scabs, not to mention that they spoke in a foreign language, assured the Italians of an

The carts of peddlers and street vendors often left huge piles of garbage standing at the end of the day. By the early 1900s, thousands of pushcarts choked the streets of the City. Conditons were unsanitary, and children who typically played on the street had less space to do so. The carts themselves, many of which were rented for as little as 25 cents a day by itinerant peddlers, posed one more obstacle to cleaning the streets.

even worse fate as a wave of resentment toward "aliens" broke out in the 1890s, not just in New York but across the country. In March 1891 eleven Italians were lynched in New Orleans in the aftermath of a labor dispute. Theodore Roosevelt, informed of this and asked his opinion, said that he thought it was "a rather good thing."

Considered "unskilled laborers," they were not welcome inside the trades-oriented AFL. Overworked, low-paid, aggrieved, and with no place else to go, they paid their dues instead to a more radical labor organization, the Knights of Labor, a union that also accepted women and blacks.

Waring "Uses" the Italians

The prevailing resentment toward Italian immigrants only added to existing tensions between the Irish and the Italians in the Department, a situation that had been festering for more than ten years before Colonel Waring came along. Despite civil service reforms, extras were not required to take the civil service examination. Waring took full advantage of this loophole and continued the Department's policy of using Italians as extras. The Colonel added to the hostility between the Irish and the Italians on the force when he announced that by importing cheap labor [the Italians] from other cities in place of citizens, he was "improving the citizenship of the city [New York]."

One week after this proclamation, the Central Labor Union ripped Waring:

> **Colonel Waring is rapidly gaining a reputation as a scab Street Cleaning Commissioner... He seems to want to reduce workingmen as low as possible, for he said that he could get men to work at $45 a month. Is the city going into the business of cutting down the wages of workingmen?**
>
> **Let him begin by reducing his own salary!**

The Union, referring to Waring's salary of $4,000 a year, also advised the Commissioner "to begin cutting down expenses by riding on a bicycle instead of an eight-hundred and fifty-dollar carriage." In conclusion, the Central Labor Union resolved that it "strongly condemns the unfeeling and malevolent expression of this high-salaried commissioner..."

Waring responded by forbidding Street Cleaners to join the Central Labor Union.

Italian Laborers Rise Up

By 1898, when the metropolis of New York took on its current distinct shape composed of five boroughs, Italian Americans made up more than a third of the municipal street cleaning force. That percentage would increase sharply over the next few years. But immigration from Italy skyrocketed at the turn of the century. By 1900 there were approximately 150,000 residents of Italian extraction living and working in the city, and their voice was starting to be heard in new quarters, especially during the labor actions of the early 1900s.

Payoffs and sweetheart deals between business and government were exposed in 1905 and, in 1906, less than a decade after Colonel Waring had set such high standards, the trail of scandal and filth led directly to the door of the Department of Street Cleaning. Thus the department marked its first quarter-century of existence by suffering the embarrassment of having its Commisioner, John Woodbury, removed due to charges of corruption.

The public held out high hopes for the new Commissioner, MacDonough Craven, who had originally been hired by and worked under Waring. But Craven lacked the vision and ability of Waring and so the Department continued to plod along, business as usual.

Craven's honeymoon period did not last long, as poor results for snow removal and garbage collection soon made him unpopular with the public and especially with the Women's Municipal League. These women who formed the upper crust of New York society had grown even more powerful since Josephine Shaw Lowell had first taken an interest in the welfare of the city's Street Cleaners.

Once again, "the women's movement" focused public attention on the city's Street Cleaners. The Women's Municipal League's progressive goals had led them first to the cause of child labor and the welfare of working women, but their campaign for sanitary reform had also made them fast friends with and defenders of the White Wings. The group saw poor worker morale at the heart of the department's inefficiency. They also railed against the payoffs rampant in the city's hiring system, and demanded better training for Street Cleaners. These mainly upper-class women saw "municipal housekeeping" as an extension of their role at home, and which allowed them to view the streets as "the hallway of the city."

Although the public also used the condition of the streets as an indicator of how well city government was working, it did not, however, share the League's concern for the welfare of Street Cleaners. Whatever measure of respect had been gotten through the efforts of Colonel Waring soon vanished. No matter what the underlying reasons were, and despite the exposure of scandal at the highest level of the department, dirty streets meant one thing to the public: the labor force charged with cleaning them was not doing its job.

This maligning of Street Cleaners was fueled by another slight, equally undeserved, that was taking place at the time: a distrust of immigrants and in particular, "the Italians." Public attitudes toward "the labor question," negative to begin with, grew vicious when combined with the growing hate-mongering directed toward these new comers.

By 1907 there were 450,000 people of Italian descent living in New York City. The newcomers tended to fall into the same occupation as their paesani and in this way assured a continuing supply of ready labor for the Street Cleaning Department. By 1906, more than half the workforce was of Italian extraction.

The difficult position of the Street Cleaners, of Italian extraction or not, was compounded by the fact of who they worked for. City workers, it was hoped anyway, would not rise up to bite the public hand that fed them. There was no latitude given civil servants, despite the fact that labor's gains in private industry clearly was not carrying over to the public sector. For the majority of citizens and government officials, the idea of municipal unions was unthinkable. Firemen and police (despite the formation of the Patrolmen's

The Street Cleaners Strike of 1907 provided a display of solidarity not just for Labor, but for the City's entire population of Italian immigrants. Here a garbage truck has defiantly dropped its load in the middle of the street, while the citizens, among them a policeman, look on.

Benevolent Association in the 1890s) were still decades away from finding their own labor voice.

The Street Cleaners Strike of 1907

The Street Cleaners Strike of 1907 became a major statement for all City workers heading into the twentieth century. The Drivers and Sweepers made a show of strength for Labor as well as for the Italians and Italian-Americans who were coming of age in the city. The Strike of 1907 started as a small job action and spread in intensity over eight days.

It was only fitting that the Street Cleaners were about to become the battering ram of the municipal labor movement. In their isolation; in their white duck uniforms; in their wages that, as of 1906, had been stuck at about $2 a day for ten years; in their lack of a pension (compared with the pensioned police and firemen); in their stuck identity as immigrants, branded as simply "the Italians," "Irish," "Jews" or "Negroes" for whole generations before the status of "Americans" would ever be conferred upon them; in their exclusion from the trade- and craft-oriented AFL and in their rebounding to the most radical and militant labor unions (the only ones that would have them); in the low-status that was accorded their jobs; in their vulnerability to the harmful effects of the Departmental policy of bringing in "extras" and their inability to end it; in the growing hazards of their jobs – now having to dodge automobiles as well as horses and carts; in the nature of the material they handled all day – garbage, rubbish, ashes and manure; in each of these things could be seen incubating a powerful new strain of unionism.

The city's continuing hodgepodge of contracting out certain parts of the city (in particular, south of Fourteenth Street) and specific elements of waste disposal (scow trimming) provides another key to understanding the early organizing of Street Cleaners. Because of this situation, city Street Cleaners faced constant exposure to, and competition with, their counterparts who worked for the private contractors and who were being organized into different unions. Unorganized scowmen for the city could not help but be influenced by the organizing efforts going on among the scowmen working for private contractors who were hauling the same city garbage. Also, the City's policy of hiring "extras," especially for the dangerous and low-paying job of scowman, meant that the Department was most certainly hiring men who had at some point joined "private" unions. Street Ccleaners were being organized from the inside as well as the outside.

A poor job of snow removal in the winter of 1906-1907 had landed criticism on the Department and, by implication, the Street Cleaners. Accusations of graft in the Department helped arouse the public's ire. In March 1907 Commissioner Craven announced that there was graft in the Department and that it was hard to stop.

The Women's Municipal League stepped in to criticize the Commissioner and to once again take up the cause of the workers. The women lent support to the Street Cleaners who were petitioning Commissioner Craven to allow the establishment of a sick fund and pension association among themselves. The petition stated that the money for the fund would come from picnics, annual balls and theatre benefits. The Department frowned on such benevolent funds, and later at the protective associations that formed among Street Cleaners, and at anything, in fact, that bore any resemblance to a union. The benevolent funds amounted to little more than organized begging. It was not the begging that bothered the Department; it was the organizing among a workforce that the bosses would have preferred to remain fragmented and isolated.

Lagging collections and cleaning marked the spring of 1907. Then, as summer approached, the men stepped up their demands, starting with a limit of 48 hours to the work week. The Department would not consider it. To make matters worse, on June 24th Commissioner Craven announced that the Department was investigating what it called the illegal solicitation of pension funds by the Drivers, Sweepers and Hostlers' Benevolent Association. As meager an effort as this was to create an "old age fund," the Department was nonetheless trying to either crush or control it. The Times, reflecting the attitude of the bosses, called it "unauthorized benevolence."

Embittered by the lack of action addressing their pay demands and at the overzealousness with which the Department scrutinized their attempts to created a pension, a total of 350 drivers walked off the job on June 25th. Another major issue of the strikers was that of unaddressed grievances. The job action was not treated seriously by the Department at first, and it was assumed the men would return to work shortly. But the Street Cleaners, after the first day, decided to join the Teamsters, an organization with considerably more experience in the way of job actions.

It was then that the City reacted with a decision to bring in scabs from other Departments and from other cities. Within no time certain streets turned into a war zone. The scabs, along with the police who escorted them, were stoned and had rotten fruit and eggs thrown at them by friends, relatives and supporters of the Street Cleaners. Further violence flared up against a backdrop of thousands of street fires as residents took to burning their own garbage. Not just stones but bombs were thrown as the situation grew more heated, especially in the Little Italy section of East Harlem.

As of day five of the strike, the City Charter contributed to the turmoil. It declared that any worker on strike for five days automatically lost their job. This only added to the Street Cleaners' desperateness and sense of abandon as the strike dragged on into its sixth day. The Times reported on the tenseness and violence of the situation as scabs attempted to haul away garbage:

> **The same police protection was provided for the men as on Sunday. Under Inspector Burns and Capt. McDormott 400 patrolmen were massed in the district and every cart had a policeman marching with swinging nightstick on either side.**

> **In the afternoon... a number of the "Italian bombs" ordinarily used for harmless fireworks display were thrown at the Street Cleaners [scabs]. One came from a roof at the corner of 107th Street and First Avenue, half an hour later another came crashing down from the corner of the same street and Second Avenue.**

The strike ended on the eighth day when the Street Cleaners obtained promises by the Department to consider the 48-hour work week, 25 cents an hour for overtime worked after that, and for fines to be imposed on Street Cleaners only after a hearing. This last item had been a major source of grievances for the men.

Hundreds of carts were immediately dispatched for the cleanup after the strike. The men went about it cheerily, in the hopes that their demands would be met. But in the coming months, the Department made only a slight adjustment in its policy of hearing grievances, and pay increases lagged behind for years to come, as did the notion of a 48-hour work week.

Commissioner Craven resigned one week after the strike ended.

Shortly after the strike, an editorial in the Times urged the City to explore the option of private contractors to collect the garbage so as to "insure against future garbage strikes." It also went on to advocate incineration, as if that were the answer to the labor problems in the Department: "The public demands that this modern municipality incinerate its own waste."

Labor unrest continued to grow during the second decade of the century and it was in March of 1911 that the tragic Triangle Shirtwaist Fire took place, killing 146 garment workers. But the municipal yoke still hung heavy around the necks of city workers. Mayor Gaynor controlled labor relations with a heavy hand which perhaps helps to account for why he was shot by a disgruntled dockworker in 1910.

Street Cleaners tried to mount another major strike again in 1911, but this time they were unable to muster support from the teamsters and sufficient solidarity among the many divisions of drivers, sweepers, laborers and hostlers, both regulars and extras. An economic depression, the Panic of 1910-1911, also weakened their cause, as the Department was able to at that time get thousands of extras at the snap of a finger. The City continued to focus on the cure-all of incineration, while labor organizing among Street Cleaners got ready to jump from the frying pan into the fire.

Chapter Four

The Promise of Productivity (and a Pension)

"If labor is a to be a commodity in the United States... it means that we shall become a nation of boarding houses instead of homes."
- President Franklin D. Roosevelt

"You can't compare conditions here with anywhere on earth."
- NYC Mayor Jimmy Walker, Dec. 20, 1928,
on the need to hire more Street Cleaners.

The new century got noisy. The clatter of metal trash cans became a fixture in an urban orchestra of honking, ringing, buzzing and clanging automobiles, telephones, elevated trains, and metalworkers taking the city in the only direction left to grow, skyward. And from there, too, would soon be heard a new roar. The Wright Brothers had figured out that they did not need more power in order to get their plane off the ground: they only needed to do a better job controlling the power they already had.

So it was with the American labor movement. Thousands of strikes, boycotts and lockouts throughout the 1880s and 1890s had amply demonstrated union power, but in the aftermath, workers often found themselves only marginally better off. And whatever progress they achieved came at a bloody price as the bosses adopted new and more brutal tactics. Where police might previously have been called in, now Army troops and state militia were summoned; night sticks and brass knuckles gave way to guns and rifles. The lack of any New York or Federal laws dealing with union organizing gave employers a free hand in putting down labor unrest. During the first years of the century management also concocted the "open shop" policy – a thinly veiled strategy to demolish union gains of the previous decades. An open shop was supposed to mean a place of employment where workers were not required to join the union, but that was just a cover for a workplace where it was made clear to workers that if they wanted the job, they should not join a union and that they would be forced to work whatever number of hours and under whichever conditions the bosses determined. The open shop was a blow to unionism.

Workers throughout the country learned the hard way that they could control their fate better with fewer strikes and more conciliation and arbitration. In New York City, the ultimate goal for Street Cleaners – and all municipal employees – remained the achievement of effective collective bargaining, but that would continue to elude them for decades to come, since it required something City Hall and the Department were still unwilling to them: a voice equal to their own.

Another Day Older and...

Although heads had been cracked and bombs thrown during the Street Cleaners' Strike of 1907, municipal labor relations were rarely as violent as those in the private sector where huge profits were at stake.

The violence that did enter the lives of Street Cleaners usually occurred on the job. For one thing, the condition of the Department's vehicles and equipment was prehistoric. For another, drivers and sweepers by the 1910s were forced to dodge not one, but two modes of bone-crushing traffic: horses and carts, as before, combined with the new hazards posed by cars and trucks. In 1914 the streets were populated by more than 100,000 horses and tens of thousands of automobiles and trucks, all vying for free lanes and parking.

Through the 1920s and 1930s, rarely did fewer than a half-dozen men die on the job each year, and thousands more were injured. In 1925 alone, 19 Street Cleaners died on the job, and more than 4,000 were injured.

The wages of Street Cleaners did not reflect the dangers of the job, and the meager pension – started only in 1913 – added insult to injury. In 1915, the City was paying Sanitationmen only $740 per year when, according to its own study, the effective yearly "minimum wage" was $820. Wages continued to sink from there. In 1918 the New York Times reported that "the average yearly expenses of a street cleaner are given as $1,367.20 and the yearly salary $939, leaving a deficit of $428." At the time, sweepers earned $3 a day and drivers, $3.50. The article went on to state that

> **Some of the working conditions are as follows: A driver does not receive any pay for overtime. He must work an hour and a half in the Summer time and in the Winter from one to four hours' overtime without compensation. If a sweeper works on Sunday he receives 30 cents an hour and for a weekday 35 cents an hour.**

More Street Cleaners were working more efficiently, but making less

The photo casts one man against a mountain. It also reflects a basic fact of garbage: that it can be weighed and measured. This fact allows collection to be quantified, making closer management possible and allowing the Productivity Program to be constantly assessed in terms of effectiveness and efficiency.

money. It was symptomatic of Labor's struggles at the time. William Green, the President of the American Federation of Labor, in a long article in the New York Times, spelled out the problem, along with his union's new position listing productivity as an important rationale for future negotiations with management:

> **Wages had not increased in proportion to output. Between 1899 and 1919 wage-earners contributed a 26% advance in productivity, but received only a 4.2% increase in their real wages. The discrepancy in the next decade was continued: a 54 % increase in productivity was rewarded with a 36% increase in real wages.**

> **Meanwhile, what had become of the vast wealth... ? The answer is not far to seek: it had been distributed in large proportions to the higher-income groups.**

Vast wealth may not have been in the cards, but Street Cleaners were definitely counting on better pay and working conditions, along with the

43

hope for a pension. Police had received pensions since 1857; by 1885 fire and police both had half-pay pensions after 20 years service. Street Cleaners had to wait until 1912 before the first fund was established under Mayor Gaynor who, ironically, had been shot and seriously wounded by an aggrieved city employee in 1910. That pension for Street Cleaners got them half pay after they had worked the job for twenty years and had reached the age of 60. Unfortunately, many never made it to 60 after 20 years on the job and, of those that did, a full 10% died within one year of retirement.

The City's pension system was poorly designed and by 1914 it was announced that it was underfinanced and headed for bankruptcy. The jumble and instability of the pension funds would continue to haunt City employees for decades to come.

Street Cleaners were taken less seriously than police, fire or teachers, but that only spurred them on to organize better. Just as the nature of their job was to pick up after everyone else, so they learned to pick themselves up, especially in pursuit of the same pay and benefits as their uniformed brothers.

And their supporters, at least in 1927, included Street Cleaning Commissioner Alfred A. Taylor who described the job of Street Cleaner as more hazardous than that of a policeman or a fireman, with one out of every four "White Wings" injured annually.

Some protection was on the way in the form of Workmen's Compensation legislation, but that was slow in coming and only sporadically adopted by various states between 1910-1920. The "labor" organizations inside the Department could do little more than politely lay their grievances at the door of the Commissioner. For, although the union movement was on the march, it showed up primarily in the form of benevolent or protective associations, which were sometimes derisively called "company unions." In 1929, the same year that the Department of Street Cleaning was renamed the Department of Sanitation, the Joint Council of the various protective associations asked for a $250 annual raise for Street Cleaners. The Joint Council also pointed out the hazardous nature of the occupation and demanded the right to retire – at any age – after 25 years on the job.

The City Changes the Rules

After the Stock Market Collapse of 1929, all the rules changed. In the stroke of a pen, City Hall rewrote the City Charter in 1929 and, in so doing, reneged on its pension commitments, leaving Street Cleaners high and dry. It would take them another 45 years to regain what they had before 1929.

Everything either went into a state of flux in the 1930s or got put on hold. The Department's makeover, with its name change from Street Cleaning to Sanitation, included the incorporation of the Street Cleaning Bureaus of Queens and Richmond counties into one larger central administration. It also introduced a new uniform, green in color. Finally, the Department attempted to impose more order with the announcement that it was going to eliminate the various job titles of sweeper, driver, and laborer, all of which would be replaced by just one title – Sanitationman.

In the face of massive unemployment during the Great Depression, the City put to work 14,000 men in the 1930s and when it snowed, as many as 40,000 extras were hired. This sudden influx of new-hires and extras weakened any new-found solidarity and diluted the organizing efforts by unionists in the Department. It also led to the proliferation and fragmentation of many different organizations and protective associations. For a management whose policy was to "divide and conquer," it helped ward off the threat of union power for municipal employees.

The City bosses were also aware of the sharp rise in labor actions and strikes in the private sector during the 1930s and wanted no part of it in municipal labor relations. Workers had been held back for too long and took a stand (many did the opposite, also, as it was during the Thirties that the "sit-down strike" was introduced). Many in the labor movement realized they had shortchanged themselves with the AFL and Samuel Gompers' philosophy of "a fair day's pay for a fair day's labor." That position was made abundantly clear by facts and statistics on the cost of living, and increases in wages versus productivity supplied by the Labor Bureau and other government organizations.

Workers did not need statistics to tell them they weren't keeping up with the cost of living. A paycheck that put less food on the table at the end of each week said it plainly. And if that was not clear enough, the stark new reality of the Depression read like a giant billboard over the labor landscape, with a message to organize, or else.

It was in this atmosphere that the more radical Congress of Industrial Organizations (CIO) had risen up in contrast to and in competition with the slower-moving and conservative American Federation of Labor (AFL). And the CIO started to do something that the AFL had failed to do – reach out to employees in the public sector.

Sanitationmen, ever pragmatic, were ready to listen to anyone that could help.

For the same reasons that they had been drawn to the radical Knights of Labor leader Terence Powderly forty years earlier, Sanitationmen in the 1930s turned to a Socialist for help. Louis Waldman was a labor lawyer who, while still in his twenties, had been elected Assemblyman, and then thrown out of the New York State legislature for his allegiance to Labor and the Socialist Party. He continued as an advocate for many civil servants, and became a leading spokesman for transit workers. Waldman was the chair of the state's Socialist Party when he was enlisted by the Joint Council in the mid-1930s to help them organize themselves from protective associations into more effective unions.

They were a little late, however, as a young firebrand named John DeLury, a laborer in a Department incinerator in Queens, was already busy organizing what was to become the one lasting union of all the city's Sanitationmen.

The long metal pole could be used by Incineratormen for picking through garbage in search of metal objects for the war effort during World War II, or for locating other objects determined of value by the Department – or the men.

Chapter Five

Where But in Hell?

"Your problems are different from those in any other department. Make this organization your organization by joining now. We want 100% Incinerator membership."

- Leaflet in 1939 encouraging laborers in the City's incinerators to join the Association of Employees of the Incinerators.

"Add to this unpleasant picture rats fat as cats running over and through the heaps of garbage, sometimes attacking the man."

- Carmine Yorio, organizer and Incineratorman.

The Department of Sanitation bore a shiny new name in 1929, but its equipment remained pitifully antique. In 1936, Sanitationmen were still driving relics from the early 1920s. Many of the older trucks jolted along on hard rubber wheels. Heating in trucks and snow plows was often non-existent, while poor ventilation caused many cases of sickness and deaths from carbon monoxide poisoning. And in the dim recesses of the city's eleven incinerators, dangerous conditions became life-threatening as a result of the Department's failure to provide safety equipment. More than one Incinerator Worker had died from inhaling noxious gases and several had burned to death in the incinerators. Another word for incinerator at that time was "destructor," a more archaic term but perhaps more appropriate given the human toll on the employees of incinerators.

Another hand-me-down characterizing the Department at that time was graft. Department higher-ups confessed to "snow racketeering" in a scandal that involved skimming money from the pay of temporary employees hired for snow removal duty. In one garage alone in 1928 they pocketed a quarter million dollars. These misdeeds further alienated a workforce piling up a mountain of grievances, with nowhere to take them. Colonel Waring's labor-management committee was a distant memory. There was no job security at the time and if a worker was brought up on charges before the Department, he was allowed no counsel unless he was a veteran of the Spanish American War of 1898 or the Great War of 1917-1918.

Street Cleaners or, as they were coming to be called, Sanitationmen, knew that they had to fend for themselves. What the Department would not do for its men, the men and their families attempted to do for themselves, typified by events like that of Sunday afternoon, August 30, 1936, when the Joint Council of Sweepers and Drivers held their annual Death Benefit Fund Picnic. A crowd of 10,000 was expected, but 14,000 Street Cleaners, friends and family turned out. The numbers spoke more about the need for a death benefit than about its success as a social event.

The premiere annual fundraising event took place every August and featured the sanitation baseball team, the "White Wings," up against either the police team, "True Blue," or the firemen's team, "Fire Nine." It was described as a "municipal classic that had taken on all the aspects of a world series rivalry." These games drew up to 50,000 spectators and were played at either Yankee Stadium or the Polo Grounds. Tickets cost $1 for box seats. In this manner, the Sanitationmen raised and split as much as $30,000 for their Welfare fund. The money went to the families of Sanitationmen who had been killed in the line of duty.

A Stepchild Named Sanitation, A Truck Named "Man-Killer"

As Mayor LaGuardia welcomed new Commissioner William F. Carey in 1936, he conceded that the Department was still a "stepchild" among the City's departments and supported Carey's attempts to buy new equipment. Sanitationmen at the time worked in teams of threes and had to lift metal trash cans filled with garbage, carry them to the truck, and then hoist them to the man on top of the truck. On this, the Mayor remarked: "Imagine having trucks in the service which require a man to lift a heavy barrel six feet higher than necessary. I want to promise you men of the department that we will get in modern equipment just as soon as we obtain the money with which to buy it." LaGuardia called the Department's old-style truck a "man-killer" and promised: "The next consignment of trucks to the City of New York will contain the self-loader."

LaGuardia's new commissioner agreed. Carey said that

We have in this department, carried on our books as equipment, over 1,800 trucks for street cleaning which, generally speaking, are nothing more nor less than pure junk. I venture the opinion

**that there isn't an equipment or junk dealer in the United States
that would pay $200 apiece for the whole lot. If there is, I would
like to have him come forward. A lot of this equipment is over
fourteen years old and for some of it we can't even get repair
parts.**

The Department had only recently been able to free itself from the era of
horse-drawn garbage carts. Now, in the midst of the Depression, money for
new equipment was hard to come by. The decrepit condition of those trucks
comes across in a request in 1936 by the Chauffeurs and Auto Truck Drivers
Protective Association, one of the four members of the Joint Council, which
asked the Department in 1939 "that windows be installed in the old-type
trucks to protect drivers from the weather."

Commissioner Carey realized the need to improve morale among Street
Cleaners. There were small steps like having new uniforms designed. But
Carey's first major attempt to turn the Department into a winner – by pushing
for the purchase of $1 million of modern snow removal equipment in the fall of
1936 – got stymied by city politics. From their point of view, Street Cleaners
had seen other well-intentioned commissioners and mayors come and go with
no lasting results. They had been beaten down too often to expect much from
a simple changing of the guard.

A reformer, Carey also had to fight the basic management attitude of the
time: that human labor was cheap, expendable and readily replaceable. Right
into the 1930s the Department was still forcing men to work 10-12-hour days
– including Sundays – without overtime. A workweek total of 72-84 hours was
not unusual. It was only in 1936 during Carey's first year as Commissioner
that the work week was reduced to 48-hours – six 8-hour days. This was the
City's response to Sanmen's demands for a 42-hour workweek of six 7-hour
days. Just the same, though, the Department continued its policy of "speed-
ups" – a term used to describe forcing a worker to perform at an intensified
pace and sometimes for longer hours – whenever collections got behind.

A Brood of Unions

By the 1930s, there were twenty-one different unions and protective
associations competing for membership among the city's 13,500 Street
Cleaners. It was a jig-saw puzzle as to who was representing which men and
for what. There were several reasons for this. Job classification of drivers vs.
sweepers vs. laborers and even the geography of the city – five boroughs each
with their different needs and priorities – all carved things up.

Another reason for the fragmentation was that the Department wanted it
that way. The last thing the City wanted was one strong union that it would
actually have to deal with in a consistent and honest fashion. As one young
labor leader, Jack Bigel, wrote looking back at that era:

With more than one union present, there could never be genuine collective bargaining. With more than one union, the full impact of Sanitationmen's power could never be felt. As long as there was more than one, City representatives could and did play one against the other. It was an elementary application of the Britannic formula – divide and rule.

The four big "departmental associations" at that time included

- Sweepers Protective Association of Manhattan and Bronx
- Sweepers Protective Association of Brooklyn
- Drivers and Sweepers Association of Queens
- Chauffeurs and Auto Truck Drivers Association in Manhattan, Brooklyn, Richmond and the Bronx.

These four groups – whose presidents were known as the "Four Horsemen" – had formed a central committee, the Joint Council of Sweepers and Drivers in an effort to gain greater clout. But without real grievance machinery or ability to collective bargain, their power was limited and their actions amounted to little more than begging.

From Ashes to Agitators

With so many groups and associations affiliated with the employees of the Department, no one paid much attention when yet another Sanitationmen's Union formed and held its first get-together at the Knights of Columbus Hall in Long Island City on the evening of Saturday, August 5, 1939. Its awkward-sounding name – "The Association of Employees of Incinerators," did not prevent it from realizing an amazing turnout for its first big function. The union had anticipated a crowd of 350; instead, 700 Incineratormen and guests showed up. No one would have given odds that night that this new group of workers banding together would – seventeen years later – become the last to stand among the dozens that had vied for the position of becoming the "one union" to represent all New York City Sanitationmen.

In 1941 – when its annual ball drew 1,200 guests – the Association of Employees of Incinerators changed its name to the Uniformed Sanitationmen's Association (USA), at which time it was still composed of Incinerator Workers. Within a few years, however, its base had expanded and it started to attract Sanmen of all stripes.

This amazing feat of leverage was accomplished by the small band of union-oriented workers who started the Association of Employees of Incinerators. One was vice-president Carmine Yorio; another was finance secretary Harry Scharaga; and then there was the most fiery of the group, the president of the new Union, John J. DeLury. Scharaga had been working as a Sanman for six years when Yorio and DeLury signed up with the Department in 1936. All

50

three worked – for $5.94 a day, six days a week – at the Ravenswood Incinerator in Long Island City, Queens.

John DeLury had made quite a jump from his previous job when he joined the Department as a dump laborer. Although in his teens he had worked for a moving and storage firm and then had tried out the vocation of pipefitter, DeLury had eventually landed work – as a courier and securities guard – at various brokerages on Wall Street. But without a college education, he was going nowhere. So at the age of thirty-two, married and with one son, the idea of a city pension appealed to him.

The job of street cleaner was physically demanding. DeLury had to show that he was capable of jumping more than just careers at that point in his life. To pass muster as a Sanman, he needed to clear a bar 3' 6" off the floor. Besides the high jump, the other physical requirements for the job in 1936 were as follows:

1) Dumbell lift – 50 pounds in one hand; 40 in the other.

2) Abdominal Muscle Lift – 25 pounds. From a recumbent position, candidates must assume a sitting position, carrying up behind his neck the dumbbell of specified weight. His legs are held.

3) Bar Chinning – Four times for a perfect score.

4) Strength of Legs – Squatting ten times with 82-pound dumbbell

5) Back and Leg Lift – Conducted on strength-testing machine

If a candidate failed the test, he looked for another job. Nobody got a second chance. The job listing issued by the Department was clear: "No physical re-examinations are granted." The physical requirements for the job grew

Incinerator Men's Ball Draws 600

The Association of Employees of Incinerators, Department of Sanitation, Forum Council No. 328, held its first annual get-together Saturday, Aug. 5, at the Knights of Columbus Hall, on 44th drive, Long Island City.

Anticipating a capacity crowd of 350, arrangements were made for the setting up of tables in the reception room in conjunction with the barroom, also the use of the second floor for dancing. At 9 p.m. the crowd grew to such proportions that extra tables had to be set up in the pool parlor and also two meeting rooms on the above floor. Instead of the expected 350, a crowd of 600 attended. More than 100 were turned away at the door, due to insufficient space, such was the success of this affair. The various committees, headed by James B. Carr and Carmine Yorio, were largely responsible for the huge success. They worked hard and devoted a goodly amount of their own time.

The association extends its thanks to Commissioner Morton, Joseph C. Zengerle, Chief Engineer, and C. H. Ketcham for their help and co-operation in making this affair possible.

The officers of the association are: John J. DeLury Jr., president; Carmine Yorio, first vice-president; Albert Neubert, second vice-president; James B. Carr, treasurer; Harry Scharaga, financial secretary; Hugh Miller, recording secretary; John Conroy, assistant secretary; John W. Lee, corresponding secretary; Henry McGrath, sergeant-at-arms; Michael Yaccarino, sergeant-at-arms.

LOCAL 831 ARCHIVES

Invitation to the "first annual get-together" of the Association of Employees of Incinerators, the predecessor to the Uniformed Sanitationmen's Association. Such balls were commonly used to help fund early pension and benefit plans.

tougher in the next few years. The Department obviously found it cheaper to make greater and greater physical demands of its workers than to purchase the modern equipment that LaGuardia promised. In fact, the physical requirements listed in 1939 had become so difficult that newspaper columnists called it the "Superman test."

DeLury started as a temporary laborer, an "extra," in 1936, and in his first six months on the job, he was laid off six times. When he did finally make it to the regular payroll, he was classified as a Sanitationman, Class A, which in the Civil Service-speak of the time meant that he was a dump laborer. "Dump laborer," however, was a broad term that covered any number of jobs at the city's open-pit dumps, transfer stations and incinerators.

Like Scharaga and Yorio, DeLury became an Incineratorman. The job description gets even more detailed from there. Scharaga and Yorio were hoppermen: they shoveled tons of refuse down a chute. DeLury was a picker: his job was to pick out any salvageable materials, especially metals, as the refuse traveled down that chute. The work was done in the dimly-lit bowels of the building. Each man tied a chain around his waste and then tied the chain to a wall or sometimes to gangs of fellow workers to keep from falling into the great fire raging below. The very oppressiveness of these conditions undoubtedly served as a fine incubator for the transformation of three workers into a trio of labor organizers.

Carmine Yorio likened a city incinerator to hell:

> Think of fires raging 1370-2000 degrees Fahrenheit. Picture a man standing on a three-foot gangplank right over these fires, chained to a wall so that he doesn't tumble into the raging inferno below...

> Then see this man surrounded day in and day out by tons and tons of garbage ridden with germs, reeking with noxious fumes and gases, and a heavy crane swinging overhead that may at any moment tumble him to immediate death, and you have the picture of a Sanitationman working an 8-hour shift as a hopperman.

> Add to this unpleasant picture rats fat as cats running over and through the heaps of garbage, sometimes attacking the man.

> If your stomach is still with you, go down to the cellar underneath the furnaces and through the haze of choking smoke, unbearable heat and the overall odor of burning garbage, [and] you will see a cellarman whose job it is to empty the furnaces of residue.

> Where but in hell will you find jobs such as these?

> The men in this Bureau are constantly haunted by the memory of four Hoppermen who, in the department's history, fell into

LOCAL 831 ARCHIVES

An Incineratorman wearing gloves – and a primitive respirator to protect against noxious fumes and smoke – uses a long metal pipe to manipulate a pole with which to open and close the incinerator door. It is easy to see why the uniform of a White Wing would not have been appropriate for this job.

the fires and were incinerated in less than a minute. These men can never forget also the three men who died only several years ago while cleaning a pit at the 215th Street Incinerator. They died not from fire, but from the poisonous gases given off by the garbage in the pit.

Yorio wrote the above words not in 1936, but in 1956 to describe the job of an Incineratorman as it still existed, and the same as he had known it two decades earlier. That nothing had changed in twenty years served as an indictment of the Department's perpetual reluctance to make improvements in working conditions for Sanitationmen.

As a witness to that same hell, John DeLury had found his true calling as a labor organizer. Coming from the environment of Wall Street, he was shocked by the working conditions he found at Ravenswood in 1936. It is fitting that one year earlier, in 1935, DeLury had taken a course in public speaking. He could not have known it at the time, but what he learned, combined with his own natural gift, was soon put to good use.

Incinerator Workers were one of the most isolated groups of workers at that time. An early pamphlet from the Association of Employees of Incinerators reads as follows:

REMEMBER: **YOUR** problems are **DIFFERENT** from those in **ANY**

53

OTHER department.

We are **FIGHTING** for **YOUR** interests every day. **HELP US TO WIN BY JOINING UP WITH YOUR OWN MEN.**

MAKE THIS ORGANIZATION **YOUR** ORGANIZATION BY **JOINING NOW.** WE WANT **100% INCINERATOR MEMBERSHIP.**

The capital letters and bold highlights reflect the original. They also reflect the energy, passion and commitment of these organizers. The pamphlet goes on to list some of the young Union's recent accomplishments, including the granting of Christmas Day as their one paid holiday, and the extension of lunch break from twenty minutes to thirty minutes in length.

DeLury's interest in labor relations and labor history extended beyond the confines of his current situation. He read history books, but more importantly he learned from veterans of labor. Inside the Department, he gained knowledge of the Department's history – and the labor movement within it – by talking to older laborers, some of whom had been on the job even before the Strike of 1911. In his writings, DeLury more than once referred to the union tradition of organizing that had begun in the Department of Street Cleaning in the 1890s.

Another person that John DeLury learned from was Louis Waldman who by the mid-1930s had been serving Street Cleaners as a spokesman and strategist for over ten years. By then Waldman was considered the best labor lawyer in New York, and he campaigned hard for collective bargaining rights for Street Cleaners. In 1937 he also argued for higher wages, a reduced work week and better working conditions for Street Cleaners and for

protecting them against arbitrary removal by their superiors by granting them the right to a full impartial hearing, with the right to be represented by counsel. The city employes can no longer be taken for granted. They cannot, in this period of labor's awakening, and growing political independence, be counted on as being in the political vest pocket of any man or any political group.

Labor-management cooperation at the time consisted of the Department listening to employees when it chose to and ignoring them the rest of the time. Street Cleaners gravitated to radicals like Waldman because they, themselves, had become radicalized by a system that gave them few options.

Sanitatiomen were deeply distrustful of the Department at that time. In 1937, as part of the changeover to the title "Sanitationman," the Department attempted a more military nomenclature, with superiors being addressed as "chief," "captain," or "lieutenant." The rank and file were to be called "privates," but that was a title which was poorly thought-out and even more poorly received, since it was the term used to describe private cartmen. It took a number of years, but finally the title "Sanitationman" started to stick. DeLury pushed for

FACTS!   FACTS!   FACTS!   FACTS!

The Association of Employees of the Incinerators of the Department of Sanitation

presents to

ALL EMPLOYEES OF THE INCINERATORS

that which we have accomplished during the short period of our existence:

1. NO man will LOSE any time because of the "slack" periods.
2. Time off with pay will be granted on Christmas Day.
3. A means of indentification has been provided for the men. Badges are being ordered at no cost to you.
4. Eight (8) days vacation IN THE SUMMER TIME.
5. Extension of Lunch Period from 20 to 30 minutes.

These and other gains have been made possible through the wonderful help and consideration shown us by our Commissioner, Deputy Commissioner and Secretary. Furthermore, we are assured of their future support because of their interest in the Labor man.

OUR PLATFORM

1) Three (3) weeks vacation in the Summer time.
2) Sick pay for those with less than five (5) years of service.
3) Time off with pay on religious holidays.
4) Better working conditions.
5) Elevate the standard of all titles in the Incinerators.

Due to the opening of the Budget around the middle of this year, we have been requested to submit those proposals which we believe to be of benefit to our men. Thus far, we have been able to arrive at a satisfactory conclusion only on the question of Dump Laborers, which proposal we now submit:

1) Dump Laborers are to be paid on the per annum basis of $1980 a year, the year being 313 days long.
2) a) Licensed Firemen in the incinerators and Oilers are to be paid $8.00 per day.
   b) Licensed Firemen and Oilers are to be paid on the per annum basis of $2347.50 per year, the working year to be 313 days long.

Note—a and b of proposition No. 2 to be decided by the Licensed Firemen pending a canvass.

We are FIGHTING for YOUR interests every day. HELP US TO WIN BY JOINING UP WITH YOUR OWN MEN.

REMEMBER: YOUR problems are DIFFERENT from those in ANY OTHER department. MAKE THIS ORGANZATION YOUR ORGANIZATION BY J O I N I N G N O W. WE WANT 100% INCINERATOR MEMBERSHIP.

All the men working in the incinerators, except those in supervisory capacity are eligible for membership. NO INITIATION FEES. Dues are only 50 cents per month.

We already have over 400 paid members!

YOUR OFFICERS:

Thomas A. Heaney, President
John A. Aylmer, 1st Vice President
Martin Norton, 2nd Vice President
Samuel Milestone, Financial Secretary
Patrick Ross McDonald, Secretary
John W. Lee, Corresponding Secretary
Harry McGrath ⎱ Sergeants-at-Arms
Michael Yaccarino ⎰
James B. Carr, Treasurer

BOARD OF TRUSTEES:

Harry Cooney

Edward Conlin

An early circular of the newly formed Association of the Employees of the Incinerators." As a new association – on its way to becoming a full-fledged union – it naturally sought to widen membership. John DeLury became one of those members and soon after that, its President.

the new title, "Sanitationman," because it elevated a "dump laborer" to a new and higher class within the civil service. He correctly reasoned that, together with the new uniforms, the title "Uniformed Sanitationman" would impart a

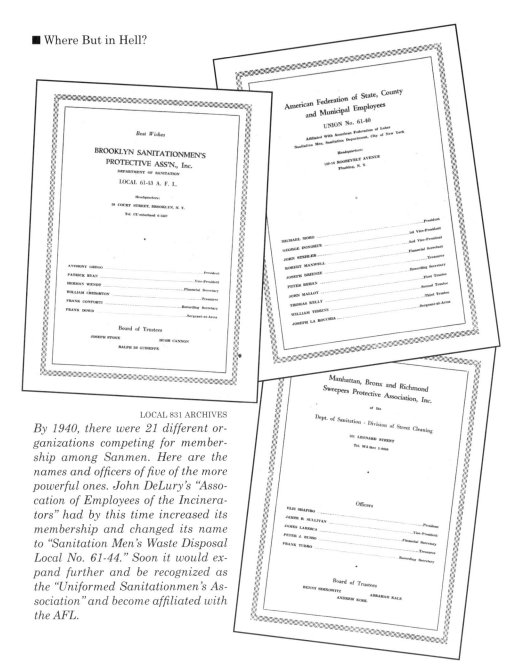

By 1940, there were 21 different organizations competing for membership among Sanmen. Here are the names and officers of five of the more powerful ones. John DeLury's "Association of Employees of the Incinerators" had by this time increased its membership and changed its name to "Sanitation Men's Waste Disposal Local No. 61-44." Soon it would expand further and be recognized as the "Uniformed Sanitationmen's Association" and become affiliated with the AFL.

real identity to Street Cleaners.

As for his own identity, DeLury soon became a full-time union organizer and leader. Many years later, the old Incineratorman and Union leader described the times:

> **Everything I ever did, I did out of sheer necessity, to protect myself and my family ... Wall Street scared the hell out of me, it was so unstable – even before the crash ... and when an opening**

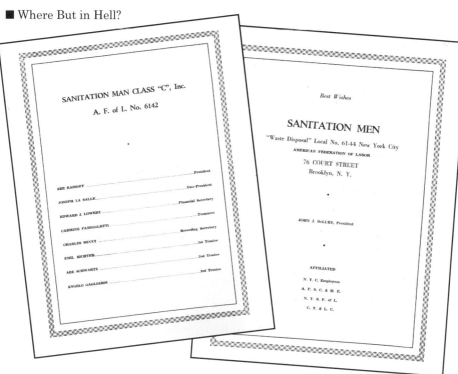

came up in the Sanitation Department, I jumped to take it. But there was no job security in the Sanitation Department – you weren't guaranteed a wage, and they could lay you off whenever they wanted. If they brought you in at seven in the morning, they could send you home at ten. And during a big snowstorm nothing was brought in to the incinerators and there was no work at all. You might get a vacation, but it would be in the winter, and only if a foreman liked you. There was a union, but it existed only to make no-show jobs for Tammany people. Legally, you could get fired for organizing a union without the commissioner's approval. So when my five friends and I got started with our thirty-six dollars, we called ourselves an association of the employees of the incinerator. The thirty-six dollars we used for carfare and lunch money when we went around talking to the men at their homes. They were fearful – organizing might get them fired – but then one of the fellows got into a jam with the department and we were able, somehow or other, to get him out. That gave us the edge, got our foot in the door. The dump laborers were the smallest end of the department – only about four hundred men – and we organized them first. It went fast – men who work with their hands respond physically and make decisions immediately.

So it was that after he had removed his own chains from those subterranean walls of Ravenswood, DeLury set about freeing all his brothers from the shackles of meager pay and oppressive conditions. Although he soon left the Queens incinerator, there continued to burn in his belly and in his eyes a fire not to be extinguished any time soon.

Better the Enemy You Know

In 1939 Commissioner Carey was thinking big. It is the only explanation for how he latched on to a novel scheme to raise morale in the Department – by purchasing a country estate for the men. And not just any one. In the name of the Department, he arranged for the purchase of a French chateau-designed estate of former millionaire Otto Hahn. Located in Woodbury, Long Island, the Hahn property spread out over 440 rolling acres and consisted of approximately (who was counting?) 100 rooms, each with its own fireplace. The complex also featured its own golf course, a private air landing strip and, of course, swimming pool. It had at one time been valued at $1.1 million, but the Depression had put the owners behind on their taxes and so they sold it to Carey for a "nominal sum." The Commissioner disclosed that he used the Sanmen's Welfare Fund to purchase it.

What he did not disclose, however, was his use of Sanitationmen to repair and renovate the estate over the next year. When this poorly hidden fact came to light, a mini-scandal arose that then got linked to Mayor LaGuardia who, it turned out, had also used the labor of Sanitationmen to work on his own place in the country.

In the end, Carey was saved from disgrace when yet one more hidden secret emerged. It turned out that the Commissioner, in his anxiousness to actually get something done in the Department, had poured over $100,000 of his own money into the property. The City nonetheless took a harder look at the whole project and then nixed it. It must not have been too big a disappointment to the Sanmen who could certainly find other air strips on which to land in their private planes or on chartered flights, and other golf courses at which to play a quick nine on their once-every-two weeks day off.

In May 1941, Carey extended "formal recognition" to five unions that had become affiliated with the American Federation of Labor. As expected, they were the four established unions of the Joint Council, and one newcomer, DeLury's small group of Incineratormen who renamed themselves the Uniformed Sanitationmen's Association. "These organizations through their joint council have petitioned for recognition as the bargaining agency for sanitation men in the Department of Sanitation. This department ... will deal with them as the representatives on problems relating to their employment."

The Department's strategy was simple and effective. By recognizing the AFL-affiliated element of the labor movement inside the Department, Commissioner Carey was able to – for the time being – shift control of workers to a union that had a clear tradition of concentrating on its craft and not on external politics. That had long been the mission of the AFL, from the time of

Samuel Gompers up to John DeLury.

This also explains the sudden prominence of the Uniformed Sanitationmen's Association. John DeLury's young union had sprung up as a result of the City's sudden emphasis on incineration. The Department needed incinerators, but it had difficulty finding laborers to work in them under those abominable conditions. The Department could fire and then replace in one day any one-thousand Sanitationmen in any other job class. Not so with Incineratormen. There weren't many men willing to take *those* jobs. A day's wage of $5.94, even in those times, was short money to face a constant risk of death by incineration. In a sense, the uniqueness of Incinerator Workers – and resulting uniqueness of their union – represented the exact opposite of the Sanitation Benevolent Association's shotgun approach to organizing. It was that same uniqueness that made Incineratormen essential to the running of the Department. It assured the USA of special consideration. Thus it was that the relatively small group of Incinerator Workers and their Union, the Uniformed Sanitationmen's Association, became the fifth member of the Joint Council.

Labor Steps Back During the War

Sanitationmen, like their brothers in the Police and Fire Departments, pulled many extra shifts and Sundays without pay in order to make up for the reduced wartime staffing. More than a thousand Sanitationmen did active military service during World War II. They felt it their patriotic duty. They could also feel the newly-tightened wartime leash of the Department.

In addition, the City mounted major campaigns for the salvage of metal – primarily in the form of cans – that added considerably to the load of Sanitation Workers.

In 1942, the first year of what was called "Salvage for Victory," the residents of New York's five boroughs collected more than a thousand tons of tin cans a month. It grew from there. Manhattan competed with Brooklyn for the highest totals. And not just tin cans. From ball bearings and safes to bed frames and Civil War swords, sanitation men picked up scrap metal at designated locations throughout the city and carted it away. A citizen's letter to the editor of the New York Times described it best:

I was rather proud of the part I played in Brooklyn's scrap-collection drive until today. Now I feel a bit humble. It is true that I sweated for an hour or so dragging the heavier stuff from the cellar to the scrap pile on my block, but that was a feeble effort compared to the work done by the Department of Sanitation men who had the job of loading those mountains of junk onto the trucks.

I watched them labor – many of them middle-aged and beyond – and my hat is off to them. Day after day in borough after borough they struggle with heavy metal objects that were certainly not included in the contract when they were hired. This is their contribution to the war effort at this time and it is one that puts to shame the things that many of the rest of us are doing. The community owes them a vote of thanks, and this is my attempt to see that they get it.

The letter was dated October 8, 1942 and signed by Martin Panzer of Brooklyn.

During the war, the Department continued to have snow removal problems, but for a very different reason: the Army had commandeered much of the Department's snow removal equipment for use in Russia and "at various other points" overseas.

The war ended in 1945. LaGuardia served out his third term and William O'Dwyer became New York City Mayor in 1946. O'Dwyer, like the fiery Transport Workers Union President Mike Quill, had also been born in Ireland, but that did not keep Quill from expressing outrage when Mayor O'Dwyer proposed doubling the nickel fare for city transit to a dime. Meanwhile, a Local 333 of the CIO had formed among Sanitationmen and, in alliance with Quill, it also protested the increase. The fare went up anyway. For the next five years, Local 333 continued to rant and rail against the Mayor, and accusing him of serving as front man for the Democratic Tammany organization.

Compared with their CIO brothers, the five sanitation AFL locals that made up the Joint Council of Sweepers and Drivers stepped more cautiously in their approach to the City. They got rid of the words "sweepers and drivers" from their name and changed it to the Joint Board of Sanitation Locals. By this point John DeLury was making it clear that, although he sat on the Joint Board as its fifth member, he had no interest in playing fifth wheel.

In 1946 DeLury got his chance to become a major player when the head of the Bronx branch of the Joint Board, Abe Kasoff, got busted by Commissioner Carey for mishandling dues. Kasoff was forbidden from engaging in organizing activities inside the Department and deprived of the ability to discuss grievances with Department officials. With Kasoff essentially removed from the picture, DeLury moved in with his Union and organized Kasoff's members. It was then that he became a junior executive on the Joint Board and soon, it's de facto head. At the same time, he remained president of the Uniformed Sanitationmen's Association, still composed largely of Incinerator Workers and laborers. The USA moved its headquarters to Brooklyn. From its beginnings in Queens to the Bronx and now to Brooklyn, DeLury's base of power spread and grew. This was critical since, no matter how great his dedication to the cause of Sanmen, DeLury and his small Union of Incineratormen were going nowhere without a substantial increase in membership. As would hold true throughout the USA's history, a necessary condition for success was to produce the numbers.

Chapter Six

The Road to One Union

"Fellas, labels belong on beer cans, not on people."

> – John DeLury, defending USA consultant Jack
> Bigel, accused of being a Communist.

The years immediately after World War II are often painted prettily, with hope and optimism. True, 1946 was the first full year without war or depression in eighteen years. It was also the year that the Knicks moved into Madison Square Garden and Jackie Robinson broke the color barrier by signing with the Brooklyn Dodgers.

But in labor history, 1946 witnessed the greatest wave of workers' strikes the country had ever seen. Wages and benefits had been throttled by the Great Depression from 1929-1941 and World War II kept them choked until 1945. Peace, prosperity and upward mobility may have appeared within reach after the war, but Management wanted workers to stay right where they were – under its thumb. Labor rebelled. In New York, the list of striking workers' unions was long and varied: truckers, tugboat operators, stock exchange workers, bakers, bus drivers and washroom attendants, to mention but a few. Even the union of window cleaners struck; some called it a "brownout." Workers may have needed a rest after the war, but they were instead forced to come out fighting.

Among those looking to make up some of the ground they had lost during the war were 12,000 New York City Sanitationmen. Many of them were returning from active duty to their homes and sweethearts and, of course, their jobs.

What Jobs!

In 1946, the annual pay of a Sanitationman was just under $2,400. It was supposed to be for a 48-hour work week, six days at eight hours a day, but the Department often extended the day to nine or ten hours at no extra pay. Sundays were required at the Department's discretion and were paid at straight time. Not only was overtime not paid for occasional Sundays, but they were sometimes not paid at all as a form of penalty. The Department had also not lost its knack for spoiling Sanmen's one day of rest by calling them in to work a partial-day on Sunday. Sanitationmen at that time got three holidays a year. For the above consideration they were responsible for snow removal and for clearing and cleaning 5,000 miles of streets each day, six days a week. The daily total amounted to 5,000 cubic yards of trash. And not just trash. Their duties still included the picking up and disposal of dead animals on city streets. That year they also collected 138,555 dead cats, 82,850 dogs, 403 horses, 126 sheep, 104 rabbits, 33 hogs, 7 goats, 4 guinea pigs, 3 deer and 138 cows, the latter representing the few working farms that were still holding out in the farther reaches of Queens and the Bronx.

Noting these numbers, journalist Gilbert P. Bailey wrote in an article in the April 28, 1946 issue of the Times that

There is nothing even faintly funny about a dead cat. Yet for some whimsical reason, when 138,000 cats must be collected and hauled away, the public is inclined to smile. This all helps to make sanitation the most misunderstood job in the book.

Statistically, street cleaning is a perilous calling, perhaps more dangerous than the work of a fireman or policeman. With fiendish regularity the sanitation man is chosen by New York motorists as the man they would like most to run down. For the same reason, because he is in the street, he gets involved through no fault of his own with an inordinate number of hold-up men, suicides, fires, drownings, household emergencies and first-aid cases. The New York City citation roll for valor above the call of sanitation duty looks like a military list. Yet Hollywood has never taken the street cleaner seriously.

Government waged outright war on labor. On the federal level, a communist witch-hunt was begun. Jack Bigel, president of United Public Workers and a consultant to the Sanitationmen's CIO Local 333, would soon be claimed as one of its victims. The State, meanwhile, wrote new legislation in an attempt to curb labor. The Condon-Wadlin bill, made into law in 1947, threatened the firing of any public employee who went on strike or in any way curtailed their assigned work load. Condon-Wadlin would prove so severe as to be unworkable and, in the end, unenforceable. TWU leader Mike Quill spoke for all the city unions when he said: "There are a thousand ways around the Condon-Wadlin bill. Men have been known to get sick on

NEW YORK DAILY NEWS

The Blizzard of 1947 dropped a record 25.8" of snow on the City in one night. Like the Great Blizzard of 1888, it reminded the City of the vital work of Sanitationmen in snow removal. It was also an influence in the decision to put into effect alternate side of the street parking in 1950.

Mondays. Thousands more could get sick on Tuesday, and if there's a cat to be skinned, we can skin it from both ends."

Sanitationmen did not take any serious job actions immediately after the war and instead gave Mayor O'Dwyer the opportunity to deliver on some of his campaign rhetoric. When the 1946-47 budget came down the line, the Joint Board of AFL Locals demanded a 35% wage increase, which would bring their wages close to $1.25 per hour. They also wanted 10 cents an hour for night work, time and a half for overtime, and double time for Sundays. But their pleas were ignored by O'Dwyer, who was a big fan of the Police Department. In fact, the only time Sanmen seemed to get their fair share of publicity was when they stopped a robbery or pulled someone from a burning building. Or when it snowed.

The Blizzard of '47

Some people may have been wishing for a white Christmas as December

25, 1947 neared, but New York City Sanitationmen and their families were not among them. For it was that Christmas was their one holiday – provided it did not snow. They got the day off that Christmas and it turned out to be a fitting day of rest, since they would soon need whatever extra energy they had stored up.

The weather forecast for the day after – Friday, December 26th – mentioned possible snow flurries and strong winds for that evening. New Yorkers woke up the next morning to the heaviest snowfall in recorded history. Over 25 inches had fallen in just fifteen hours. The city froze in whiteness. Air traffic was completely blanked out. The Long Island Railroad halted operations. Thousands of cars were buried every which way on city streets. Police cars were used to make emergency runs to the city hospitals. Before it was over, the storm had claimed 77 lives and the Fire Commissioner declared it the greatest emergency in the history of the Fire Department.

More than 14,000 Sanitationmen, including 2,000 "extras," went to work in that storm. Armed with shovels and antiquated snow plows, they set about carving and clearing some narrow passage for the city's seven and a half million residents. Sanmen, especially those who worked any distance from home, spent the next two weeks sleeping in the Department's garages. Eventually they were reinforced by 30,000 temporary laborers, and got the job done.

New York had seen nothing like it since the Great Blizzard of 1888 and the city stood grateful, once again, to the "heroes of winter." This set the stage for Sanmen to continue their push for collective bargaining and use their recent snow removal successes as a chip in demanding more holidays.

But there was no real collective bargaining and so the Mayor and the Department did not need to seriously negotiate. In the end, the City agreed to but a 10% pay increase of $250 a year and just two additional holidays without pay.

And Then There Were Two

DeLury, over the ten years since he had come up from the Association of Employees of Incinerators, had displayed dynamic leadership, and a political program to go after benefits and pensions. In this way, and through constant outreach, DeLury and the Uniformed Sanitationmen's Association (USA) attracted and absorbed the membership of the other four protective associations. Now there were only two serious contenders left in the sanitation union rivalry: the USA and a relative newcomer – Local 111-A of the Building Service Employees International, an affiliate of AFSCME and the AFL that had been chartered in 1947. The president of Local 111-A, Stanley B. Krasowski, had been executive vice-president of the Joint Board in 1947, but quit when he got into a vicious fight with DeLury.

Krasowski's aggressive approach had a great appeal, especially to the younger Sanitationmen who had joined the Department since the end of

LOCAL 831 ARCHIVES

A Sanman hoists high a full metal trash can as he squeezes his way between two parked cars in the late 1950s. A job that requires part-weightlifter, part-contortionist.

World War II. By 1951, Local 111-A's membership had grown roughly equal to that of the USA, each counting about five-thousand members. Both the USA and Local 111-A claimed that a majority of the city's Sanitationmen belonged to their respective unions.

Local 111-A got more strident and militant from within. But the USA under DeLury's leadership did the opposite and reached out – to other unions and politicians. DeLury got actively involved in the AFL Central Trades and Labor Council and became good friends with its president, Martin T. Lacey, a veteran of labor organizing in New York since 1903. The older Lacey took DeLury under his wing and the two remained close friends through the 1950s. DeLury had, together with Lacey, supported Mayor O'Dwyer's reelection campaign in 1949.

Few union leaders raised the issue of respect and dignity to the level that DeLury did. He knew that that was what his men craved and that, for lack of it, morale had so often scraped bottom. It was in 1951 that he first uttered what would become for him a standard refrain: "If you want a fight, call me a garbage man!"

Of course, there were other reasons for the success of the Uniformed Sanitationmen's Association. The big prize that DeLury kept his eye on was pensions. The pension was a primary reason for his joining the Department in 1936 and pensions for Sanitationmen soon became one of his primary goals. DeLury – and ten-thousand Sanitationmen – wanted a twenty year pension, the same as police and firemen.

A Sanitationman in 1951 had to work 25 years for a pension and could not retire before the age of 55. That meant that, for the majority of Sanmen who had started working in their early or mid-twenties, it became in effect a 30-year pension, or worse. Besides, the average lifespan of a Sanitationman in the mid-1950s was only fifty-seven years. DeLury and the other executives of Local 831 constantly pointed out that the job was too physically demanding for a worker to perform for that long. The USA also wanted to increase the portion of the pension that the city paid from 50% to 75%. In 1951, Sanmen had 10% deducted from their paychecks for pensions, while fire contributed 4.9% and police just 4.1%.

DeLury, already in the early 1950s, was becoming a familiar face in Albany where he mounted a constant lobby for a better pension for Sanmen.

How to Count

The Uniformed Sanitationmen's Association raised the bar to a whole new level when they decided to join the Teamsters in 1952. The Teamsters added clout – they were the largest union not just in the city, but in the United States. Teamsters Joint Council 16 in New York had 124,000 members. Locally over the last several years, the Teamsters had flexed their muscle in a number of trucking strikes, shutting down various industries – from food supply to City services. The Teamsters had also displayed a different kind of strength – as one of the few unions in the 1950s to publicly protest the Communist witch-hunts and red-baiting of that era.

Besides, Sanitationmen *were* teamsters. They moved things, and they kept things moving in the greatest city in the world. They also commanded the largest fleet of trucks – more than 6,000 in total – in New York. And before that, it was carts – ash carts, dump carts, garbage carts. In fact, several different municipal street cleaning protective associations in the first half of the century had already been affiliated with "the Brotherhood of the Road," as the Teamsters were called.

The Teamster connection meant something to the men on the force. "I knew when DeLury joined the Teamsters ... that was it for me. I knew he was going to bring in the money, I knew we would have the power to stand up to the city and anybody else, for that matter," recounted Sanman Tony "Smash" Casalaspro. "That's when I decided to go with 831," he added, referring to the USA's affiliation as Local 831, IBT.

The fight for the 40-hour work week continued and job actions by both the

Sanmen in 1952 wear masks in order to publicize the reprisals that they risked in picketing. Here their slogans criticize the City's failure to give them a 5 day, 40 hour work week."

USA and Local 111-A were starting to win some support, including from The New York Times. In an editorial shortly after an October 1951 slowdown by Sanitationmen, the Times took a stand supporting the demand for a 40-hour week and called theirs a "just complaint" against the city:

> **Ten thousand Sanitation employees, doing hard work, are still on a forty-eight hour, six day week, when a week of such length is as dead as a dodo in American industry. How can we defend this forty-eight hour, six-day week? By saying that the city cannot afford to treat its employees equitably, in comparison with American industry?**

> **It has to come ... The question is, Will the city do it on its own motion, prompted by the conscience of a just employer, or will it have to be forced by the militant, unlawful action of disgruntled employees who beget disrespect for governmental authority by their example and by their victories?**

67

Whips, Masks and Work Weeks

The City acted as though a work week of forty-eight hours was carved in stone. That left Sanmen with one option – to chip away at it piece by piece. Forty-eight hours got whittled down to forty-six, then forty-four and, in 1953, to forty-two hours. But the 40-hour week, like DeLury's all-important demand for a twenty-year pension, still remained elusive. Local 831 continued on its tracks in dogged pursuit.

During this period John DeLury came up with a new tactic to get his message across to the public: show and tell. On August 1, 1952, he dispatched five sanitation trucks as if they were floats in a parade. Each truck was complete with its own scene: the City of New York as the "Slave-driver" was depicted by one man in high hat, tails and wielding a six-foot bull whip – riding a herd of Sanitationmen chained to garbage cans. The placards on the trucks blared: "Our job is slow murder," and listed the high rates of injury, illness and job-related deaths suffered by Sanmen. DeLury announced that the "parade" would continue the entire week throughout all five boroughs.

For example, several days later, on August 7, 1952, a dozen masked men showed up and picketed the Department pier at Twenty-First Street and the East River in protest of the City's holding out on the forty-hour work week. They wore masks in order to publicize what they said would be certain "reprisal" by the Department and let be known their intention to stop tugboats from taking garbage scows out to a city landfill. The police showed up and informed them that the masks were a violation of the law. One of the masks came off and there stood John DeLury.

DeLury was not the type of leader to hide behind any mask and if he wore one, it was to underline the potential punishment for such job actions. In the early 1950s, his Union fought to get a positive message out. And it became even more of a fight because post-World War II Americans – in their blind rush for the American dream – had developed a dislike for blue collar workers. Children were told to study hard and go to college or "you'll end up a garbageman."

The USA got support from another newspaper when the Daily News started publishing a weekly full-page section titled "Gripes from Sanitationmen." The January 12, 1953 issue starts off with the following introduction:

Step out here in the gutter, mister, and shake calloused paws of some hard workers. These are your Department of Sanitation men, the guys you cuss at sunup and honk at all day. After you've heard their story, you will realize they have good cause to gripe, and maybe you'll be more understanding.

The entire page was dedicated to Sanmen speaking their minds on the different aspects of the job, pro and con. A few excerpts from the rest of the article make the point:

Michael Simone, of 1401 67ᵗʰ St., Brooklyn, doesn't like hot ashes any better than wet ashes. Sanitationmen frequently will heave a can of ashes into their truck before they realize that the can contains live coals. A fire promptly breaks out in the truck. This means a quick trip to the nearest fire station and delay in covering a route.

John Condon, of 5101 39ᵗʰ Ave., Long Island City, Queens, told of respect for his colleagues: "Seven weeks ago before I joined the Department, I didn't look twice at a Sanitationman. Now, when I'm off-duty and pass a truck, I darn near tip my hat."

Irving Sheeger, of 19 Lewis Street., Brooklyn: And why do we have to work longer and get less pension than the cops and firemen? They can retire after 20 years, but we can't. And ours is a tougher job. Also, we get paid less than they do. Is that fair?"

In the meantime, DeLury's arch-enemy, Stanley Krasowski, quit his job as President of Local 111-A in March 1953 with the curious explanation that the by now certain arrival of the 40-hour work week had satisfied his ambitions as a labor organizer. John DeLury, however, was far from satisfied and saw those gains as mere milestones along the route to higher pay, better working conditions and, of course, his primary goal of a twenty-year pension. But before he could reach those marks, certain things and people, like the Mayor of New York City, still stood in his way.

Push Comes to Shove

Help from a new mayor was on the way. When Robert Wagner, Jr. ran for Mayor of New York in 1954 he stood out not just as a Democrat, but as a man of labor. Wagner was the Manhattan borough president and politically savvy, but even more important, he was the son of the highly regarded former U.S. Senator from New York, Robert Wagner. His father, the author of the Wagner Act in 1935, had made the name "Wagner" almost synonymous with Social Security and all things positive for labor. And Robert Wagner, Jr. gave every indication of being his father's son. This was the man for John DeLury.

In fact, Wagner announced that he wanted to go a step further than the old man by reorganizing the city's handling of labor relations and declaring the need for a similar bill of rights for public employees in New York. Far from seeing public workers as an insignificant group, Wagner accorded them respect and attention. Wagner was DeLury's man, and DeLury soon became Wagner's as the USA president, accompanied by his powerful friend Martin

T. Lacey, courted and then supported Wagner in his first bid for mayor. Wagner, in that 1953 election campaign, promised DeLury that he would support the USA's campaign for the twenty-year pension. DeLury remained determined to hold the Mayor to that promise and for years to come would remind the Mayor of it in writing, in public speeches and face-to-face.

The USA started to back up its pension demands with more statistics and medical studies substantiating the heavy physical toll that the job was taking on Sanmen's health and their lives. DeLury wrote in the Times in 1953:

> ...for years we have petitioned, implored and yes, even begged various city administrations to make an impartial study of the wear and tear on the Sanitationmen who trudge miles every day, lifting and emptying heavy barrels of refuse, operating five-ton trucks, operating incinerators, etc. Our pleas for even a study were of no avail.

> As a last recourse, this local union, which represents 95% of all Sanitation Workers, finally employed a distinguished researcher in the field of industrial diseases and physiology, Dr. Peter V. Karpovich of Springfield College. His final report... presented some startling facts – namely: that of all industrial occupations in the United States, the job of the New York City Sanitationman is the third most hazardous, exceeded only by the hazards of the logging industry and among longshoremen, and far exceeding the rate of injury sustained in police departments, fire departments, etc.

> The study will show... that it is inhumane to expect that loaders and drivers can maintain peak efficiency for the thirty-two years of employment now required before they can even consider retirement.

The Uphill Battle for a 20-year Pension

When in 1954 Wagner got elected mayor in a landslide, a new era in labor relations began for the city's public employees. Entrenched bureaucrats and career-appointed officials, however, did not disappear overnight and so, in many quarters, the old times and old ways hung on stubbornly for years.

No sooner than Wagner took office did John DeLury start insisting on real collective bargaining to take place before the next year's budget got handed down. The City's response – a flat "no."

This prompted DeLury to improvise what he called a "strikeless strike." The purpose of this job action was to get increased wages and a higher uniform allowance. The key to its success rested on a total cutting off of

THE TEAMSTERS RECORD

UNIFORMED SANITATIONMEN'S ASSOCIATION • LOCAL 831 • INTERNATIONAL BROTHERHOOD OF TEAMSTERS — AFL-CIO •••• JANUARY, 1956

SANITATIONMEN WILL VOTE FOR ONE UNION!

THE DAY IS FRIDAY, JANUARY 27th!

THESE STORIES AND PHOTOS FROM THE CITY'S NEWSPAPERS TELL WHY

THE MAJORITY OF SANITATIONMEN WILL VOTE TEAMSTERS!

From The Chief, 1-1-54

Sanitation Union Asks
Written Agreement

LOCAL 831 ARCHIVES

Teamsters Record headline for the coming election in the run-off between Local 831 and Local 111-A. Local 831 won in a landslide, becoming the one Union of all the City's Sanitationmen. This allowed Local 831 to become the first municipal union to be recognized as the sole bargaining agent in true collective bargaining with the City, a goal of Street Cleaners and Sanitationmen for 75 years, since the formation of the Department of Street Cleaning in 1881. It also paved the way for other municipal unions seeking to collectively bargain.

supplies necessary for the Department to continue operating. On June 8, 1954, Sanmen picketed Department garages and prevented gas and oil trucks from getting through. The backing of Martin Lacey's Teamsters also helped. The next day DeLury announced that no Sanititationman would drive any truck or operate any piece of equipment that was unsafe. Again, this served to freeze operations in the Department.

The Department retaliated by suddenly ordering eye examinations for 8,000 Sanmen. DeLury called it a "thinly disguised effort to place the onus of the increased number of accidents on the shoulders of Sanitationmen. The city offered a $200 yearly increase in wages, which the Union accepted. But Local 831's rank and file roared disapproval at the $20 uniform allowance granted by the City. The paltry uniform allowance – police got $125 for their uniforms – boiled over into yet another public protest by Local 831 – this time a march on City Hall in driving rain that led to it being branded for a long time to come as the "Wetback Parade."

What upset Sanmen about the uniform allowance was not so much the money. True, the $105 difference between what Sanmen and the cops got was a lot of money in 1954 (more than one week's pay for a Sanitationman), but the real reason for their anger was more about the usual unfairness of the City on issues of compensation and treatment.

The meager allowance for uniforms also underscored the indifference toward the job of a Sanman on the part of City officials. Since the time of the White Wings, the uniform of a Sanman got ripped, torn, burned through and just plain worn out, the Union maintained, with a much greater frequency than that of a policeman. If clothes make the man, then the fate of these uniforms said something about the fate of the men wearing them. These uniforms spoke volumes about the physical grind of the job. Not to give more than the $20 allowance was to ignore these distressing facts. In their way the uniforms reinforced the conclusions of Dr. Peter Karpovich – that there was a high cost to the health and welfare of this group of workers. Pensions weren't just needed – they were necessary.

The uniform issue also rang up a connection to the pension issue on another level: the continuing disparity between police and sanitation pensions. Police paid 4.1% of their salary into their pension and could retire after twenty years and as early as age forty. The City paid 50% of their pension. Sanmen at that time paid 10% of their salary, could not retire until they had put in twenty-five years and not before age fifty-five. The city paid only 25% of their pension.

"The Pension Express"

Among his more ambitious and imaginative attempts to promote the cause of a better pension for Sanmen, DeLury in 1955 organized a mass rally of the city's Sanitationmen in the state capitol. "Teamsters Fly Pension Delegation To Albany" read the caption to a photograph showing dozens of Sanitationmen about to board a plane. Another thousand Sanmen took the train, a fifteen-car special which was dubbed the "Pension Express." Dressed in their green uniforms and armed with flags and picket signs, they marched up the steps of the state capitol and demonstrated.

It took one more year of pressuring the City, but Local 831 finally got the uniform allowance to $65. It was going to take much longer to get any satisfaction on pensions.

One For All

A final showdown loomed between Local 111-A and the USA when Mayor Wagner announced that the first phase of his new labor relations setup would require different groups of City employees to decide on which one union would represent them. DeLury immediately pressed for a representation election in early 1956. Local 111-A, although it claimed a majority of the City's Sanmen in its membership, had been without a mission and lacked any agenda beyond pay raises and a shorter work week.

Since Stanley Krasowski quit, Local 111-A had experienced a real decline in numbers. It did not look to be much of a contest for Local 831. DeLury and the USA knew that they had a clear majority.

This fact was borne out on January 27, 1956, the date that the Sanitationmen of New York City chose the one union to represent them. The USA crushed Local 111-A, receiving 6,350 votes to only 2,802 for Local 111-A. Finally, the Sanitationmen of New York City were united. The Uniformed Sanitationmen's Association that had started out twenty years earlier as a small isolated union of Incinerator Workers had become the one representative and one voice for all the City's Sanitationmen.

Between lighting a cigar after the representation election – and probably a second cigar a few months later on July 1, 1956, when Sanmen finally got a forty-hour work week – DeLury and Local 831 did not get much of a break. In fact, Local 831's membership had swelled by one-third overnight with the new members absorbed from Local 111-A. The little Irishman and his band of sanitation union executives had their hands full with new demands for wage increases, benefits and, of course, a pension equal to that of firmen and policemen.

For DeLury, all of these steps – real collective bargaining, certification, and dues checkoff led in one direction – the twenty-year pension. Even Sanitation Commissioner Andrew Mulrain noted in 1956 that there were 1,200 Sanmen under 55 years of age who were on "limited duty" due to injuries.

After lifting barrels for twenty-five years they are not able to do sanitation work. I pledge to you and to your union that I will assist in any way I can to get a better pension system for the Sanitation Department, namely a twenty-year plan.

The representation election had been mainly symbolic – Local 111-A was largely dead. The real challenge ahead was for Local 831 to be formally certified as the exclusive collective bargaining agent for Sanmen. Mayor Wagner had made a major commitment to City employees, and the USA was first in line to test it. In the meantime, for John DeLury and the USA, there were other pressing matters afoot.

Mixing It Up with the Mob

As part of his overhaul of city government, Bob Wagner had set up a new Division of Administration. Its head, Luther Gulick, reported on different aspects of the city's housekeeping, including refuse removal from commercial establishments in the city. His study dated July 19, 1954, came to the following conclusions:

- overcharging and monopoly conditions was rampant among private carters
- discrimination existed on the part of the city in providing free refuse collection to 52,000 business establishments located in residential buildings
- the city should start charging these businesses – and realize savings of $10 million to $12 million annually

It was a straightforward report, with which John DeLury and Local 831 strongly agreed, that advised the city to end "free refuse removal" to commercial establishments located in residential buildings and which, as a result, enjoyed an unfair advantage over business competitors that were in non-residential buildings and who had to pay private cartmen to take away their refuse. Gulick emphatically recommended that the city start charging for this service to businesses "in the form of a utility." Not only did he point out potential savings of $10-12 million, but he listed two other reasons as well. First, his study showed that the "privates" did not have the capacity to handle the added load of 52,000 new commercial/residential accounts. And second, the private carting industry was clearly dominated by the mob and handing over that much business overnight would amount to a windfall for the gangsters. Despite these warnings, the Mayor did nothing and the City Council announced that the private cartmen would take over the commercial/residential accounts. The Mayor and the City Council stood by their projection that the City would save $6 million a year through the money that it collected from license fees. There was no analysis of the ramifications and loss of jobs and income to the City's Sanmen.

DeLury was furious. If it passed, the Sharkey Bill meant that 291 city Sanmen would lose their jobs. It was his duty to protect his rank-and-file. Local 831 submitted their own study, showing that the savings to the city would be no more than $1.4 million and that the residential/commercial establishments were far greater in number than the city's estimate of 52,000. In June 1956, two months before a statement at the Mayor's Hearing on the Sharkey Bill, DeLury submitted a written statement:

"Fools rush in where angels fear to tread" is an old folk saying. But the people who stand to profit and profit highly from this Bill are not fools.

In return for accepting minimum regulations long, long overdue, they are getting, from the City of New York, a fabulous gold mine, rivaled only by Fort Knox. In this instance, Mr. Mayor, it can truly be said that <u>GARBAGE IS GOLD.</u>

Will you explain this to me: "Why has the City so lightly refused Dr. Gulick's recommendation?"

If your figures are right, then you are giving the private cartmen a 74.28% increase in business. That, in itself, is a bonanza.

But you have been misinformed, Mr. Mayor. The figure is not 52,000. [It's] closer to 80,000. And if you check with the Department of Sanitation, you will find I am right. The actual figure is 78,500. The increase in the private cartmen's businees, therefore, is not 74%. It is greater than 100%.

As an old-time trade unionist and, therefore, as one who wishes to give all-out support to you and your administration, I respectfully urge that you reconsider the entire policy and adopt the recommendations made by Dr. Gulick in 1954.

The City did not follow DeLury's advice and on July 1, 1956, it handed over nearly 80,000 commercial/residential accounts to the private cartmen. DeLury's protests that June did not get much press. Two months later it was a different story.

In mid-October 1956 the Daily News ran a series of articles that detailed the corruption and level of criminal activity in the private carting industry in New York. Interviews with dozens of businesses revealed extraordinarily high charges for refuse removal; an inability to "shop around" because the private cartmen had so clearly allocated territories and refused to poach accounts from each other; and threats of physical violence to anyone who questioned what amounted to a cartel.

One City, One Union

The five boroughs may have been joined together as one city sixty years earlier, but many of the functions of the running of the government still operated in a localized and inefficient fashion. If the Borough president of Brooklyn had a problem with street sweeping, he called the Street Cleaning Department in Brooklyn which could then call upon the Brooklyn Protective Association which represented Brooklyn Street Cleaners. It was clunky and often inefficient. Local 831, however, now exerted centralized control over its membership. This made the union efficient and able to concentrate on quickly achieving the other landmarks that it was seeking from the Wagner administration: certification and dues check-off. This made official the automatic deduction of union dues from the check of a city employee and the payment of that amount to union. It is a simple system, but essential to the running of a modern union. Now it had been presented – and gladly accepted – as part of Mayor Wagner's city labor overhaul.

DeLury always kept his eye on pensions, the primary reason for his joining the Department in 1936. And so pensions for Sanitationmen became one of his primary goals. By the early 1950s DeLury had become a familiar face on the capitol steps in Albany, so often was he traveling there to lobby for pension reform.

And, in the process, he was gaining the political savvy that was going to serve him so well in the stormy decade to come.

Chapter Seven

Sixties A-Go-Go

"I want to thank you very much for the editorial in The Chief of Aug. 30 about the Sanitation widows whom the city expects to live on only $50 a month. We are starving, wearing other people's clothes and if we pay a bill, we don't eat. We live like beggars while food and everything else keeps going up. I can't work and I can't walk because of arthritis. I'm a widow 11 years."

- Letter to the Editor of The Chief, Nov. 1, 1963, written by a Sanitationman's widow.

In 1960, Local 831 was marking its fourth year as the one Union of Sanitationmen. Wagner was still Mayor, but when it came to labor relations, he acted more like a king. He often got involved hands-on in labor negotiations and he had a good working relationship with many union leaders, including John DeLury. But close relations with the unions, from the mayor's perspective, meant keeping them on a short leash.

Wagner never lost an opportunity to test the strength of the newly certified Uniformed Sanitationmen's Association. For every inch that he and the city negotiators gave up, they demanded a foot. Whereas Sanmen might have welcomed a portrait of themselves as a racehorse, the fact was that the city still treated them more or less as it always had, as a beast of burden.

At the end of the 1950s, New York City was changing. Industry, especially manufacturing, was leaving, headed south where wages were cheaper (and unions weaker or non-existent). Much of the empty industrial space was taken over by offices. Since NYC Sanitationmen handled only residential refuse and garbage, their workload continued to increase rapidly. Wages and benefits continued to lag.

The US space program reflected the nation's new enthusiasm. The nation's new and youngest elected president, John F. Kennedy, announced the goal of a lunar landing by the the end of the decade and a nation turned its gaze skyward.

Local 831, however, was focused more in the direction of City Hall, where it was arguing for a $416 increase in yearly salary for its members and an improvement in the pension program. Wage increases meant much to Sanmen, trying to improve their lives and at the same time achieve their long-desired parity with New York City's other uniformed services.

Pensions meant even more. Whether you were a driver, sweeper, scowman or Incineratorman, the work ground you down. What had begun as a shaky pension program fifty years earlier had only grown slowly. In 1960, 50% of pension contributions came out of Sanmen's paychecks. It was a big bite. To a Sanitationman, whose starting annual salary in 1960 was only $4,050, that 50% of the pension contribution was huge.

The case for an increased pension contribution was emphasized by Jack Bigel in a small booklet about Local 831, titled "A Union on the March":

"The issue felt most deeply in the hearts, muscles and minds of all men, was the need for drastic pension revision. Here emotions flowed deep and rose high. The cost of the pension cut sharply in the Sanitationman's ability to provide for his family. Fifteen percent and more of his gross salary was being deducted just for pensions. The amount of service on the job to enable retirement at half pay was too long."

Negotiations for the wage and pension package dragged on through the winter, spring and into summer of 1960. The Union stood firm in its demands, speaking in a unified voice through its president, John DeLury. The city sang its usual song of woe, offering only $200 in response to the requested $416 annual increase.

For 10,000 Sanitationmen, this was not enough. The discontent got louder at each steward's meeting. It soon resulted in an explosion that marked the first of two major labor actions by Local 831 during the 1960s.

The Strike of 1960

The clanging and clatter of metal garbage cans was missing in New York City on the morning of Wednesday, July 27, 1960. In the days before plastic trash cans, the sound was unmistakable: Sanmen played percussion.

But on July 27 all was quiet as some 7,000 of Local 831's members held a meeting at Manhattan Center. The first 5,000 got in. Another 2,000 had to wait outside.

John DeLury had called the 4 a.m. meeting so that the Union's rank and file could vote on the City's latest offer, which fell far short of the Union's demands for a wage increase and contained nothing for pensions.

The Sanitationmen unanimously voted down the city's offer. The men walked.

Marching on City Hall in the 1960 Strike. The civil service newspaper, The Chief, called the parade a "bargaining committee of nine thousand." In fact, it was seven thousand Sanmen who kept it an orderly and effective job action up to the point they arrived at City Hall.

DAY ONE: "Rocks in their Heads!"

The Strike of 1960 had begun. Or was it a strike? The State's Condon Wadlin law, which had been passed thirteen years earlier, was a drastic statute which would have subjected striking workers to dismissal. So, the

NEW YORK DAILY NEWS

July 27, 1960 Strike. Once they arrived at the postage-stamp size space outside City Hall, the men started getting rambunctious.

Union called it a "work stoppage"; the Mayor, treading carefully, stepped around the question when asked if he considered it a strike. Newspapers fell in line with the Mayor and called it either a "walkout" or a "garbage tie-up."

The seven thousand Sanmen who had gathered at Manhattan Center marched to City Hall. Newspaper accounts at the time repeatedly use the adjective "angry" to describe the Sanitationmen. The actual events which took place that day spoke more of determination than anger.

During the three-mile long march to City Hall, the Sanmen stayed in orderly fashion and for the most part kept to one side of the street, allowing traffic to move along. They shouted slogans, sang labor songs, and chanted "Go! Go! Go!" along the entire route.

The civil service newspaper, The Chief, put it like this: "New York City had never witnessed a spectacle such as this event which was making civil service labor history in America."

Once at City Hall more than a thousand workers from other municipal unions joined them in support. The Chief described them as a "bargaining committee of nine-thousand." John DeLury, heading the actual 60-member

Union Bargaining Committee, met with the Mayor and City negotiators. They quickly reached a stalemate when the city insisted that Sanitationmen would have to return to work in order for negotiations to continue. In the meantime, garbage was piling up on the streets at the rate of 8,000 tons a day. Sanitation Commissioner Paul Screvane assured residents that there were no immediate health hazards. The commissioner asked the citizens of New York City to stuff their garbage cans "a little tighter."

DAY TWO: Walk Softly and Carry a Crowbar

Recognizing that no progress could be made with negotiations, John DeLury reversed his position and the next day, Thursday, July 27, urged the Sanmen to return to work. This reversal took long and hard arguing as well as persuasive tactics by DeLury. Ultimately, DeLury and his bargaining committee pulled a rabbit out of the mayor's tophat. The City agreed to both the wage increase and, more importantly, to contribute an additional 2 ½% toward pensions. It was now a 47 ½% to 52 ½% split and meant another $190 in take-home pay for Sanmen.

Perhaps the coming mayoral election influenced the outcome. The Mayor knew he could only benefit from the support of the Uniformed Sanitationmen's Association. The improvement in the pension program was especially appreciated and DeLury was hoisted up onto the shoulders of his bargaining committee and cheered by several thousand Union members.

The Early Sixties – USA Builds its Own Power Base

In 1961 Mayor Wagner was nearing the end of his second term and looking at an election in the fall. Polls showed his popularity slipping. Re-nomination by the Democratic party was by no means a given.

Wagner did succeed in getting nominated, but he ran as a "reformer" and without the support of the bosses. He got elected to his third term largely due to support from the city unions which provided a large motivated base of campaign workers. Sanitationmen did their part in affecting the outcome of the election. The political landscape was changing, and municipal unions were clearly growing in power, a fact that was not lost on Wagner or other politicians.

Tell It To City Hall! – Power and Politics in the Early 60's

Mayor Wagner did more than just give legitimate status to city unions which met certain criteria. Certification (and the threat of having it removed), together with dues checkoff and the right to collective bargaining put Local 831 and the other certified city unions on more of a level playing field with City Hall. It gave the unions more power and, at the same time, consolidated City Hall's power in dealing with them. A new relationship of labor to management was forming. This new relationship lessened the power of borough presidents and district political bosses in city union matters. Now Sanitationmen had a direct pipeline to City Hall. "Go tell it to City Hall!" became a real possibility. And tell it to City Hall they did.

In addition to the new source of union power brought about by Wagner, Local 831 drew its political strength from other sources as well. In particular, it had two things going for it. One was its leader, John DeLury. The other was the way the members of Local 831 worked together.

Their name said it all: the Uniformed Sanitationmen's Association. They were uniformed, they were Sanitationmen, and their association was with each other. Of course there were many differences within the membership and certain of these, such as generational differences, caused occasional disagreements. But at their core, they were all Sanitationmen and their union, as a result, usually spoke with one clear voice.

With USA's support, Wagner won the primary in a landslide and the general election by a 2% margin.

The "Invisible Service"

Another result of Local 831's new power became apparent in a change in its relationship to the Department in which its members were employed. The Union had always sought to influence the actual working and daily operations of the Department, with varying degrees of success. How much input and how successful it was depended on such things as personnel, budget, and who was Mayor. The relationship could also turn on a dime, as commissioners came and went. Last, because some Department officials were appointed and some were career civil servants, management at times lacked quality, at other times consistency, and sometimes both.

Local 831 was constantly trying to protect and advocate for its members without the benefit of standard guidelines and human relations policies from the Department. This situation was not in the interests of Local 831. The Union and its members needed the Department to run smoothly. When the Department had problems, Sanitationmen had problems, and the results showed up immediately in a most visible location: the city streets.

If citizens see garbage on the street, their first instinct is not to question the efficacy of management; rather, they tend to shoot from the hip and point a finger at easiest and only visible target: Sanitationmen.

That is why, for example, Jimmy Alongi, a veteran from that era, describes the work of a Sanitationman as "the invisible service."

Thus Local 831 welcomed the "memorandum of understanding" presented

John DeLury gets roughed up in the 1960 Strike and must be escorted to safety by police.

to it by the Department of Sanitation in February, 1961. Commissioner Screvane signed for the Department and John DeLury for the union. The contract contained a full grievance procedure which included a guarantee of full-time representation for the processing of grievances. It also addressed the need to standardize some other important issues, such as sick leave, vacations, scheduling of overtime and hours or work.

John DeLury hailed the memorandum of understanding as a first, not only in New York City, but as a first between any union and mayoral agency in the country.

Pensions, Pensions, Pensions

Armed with new power at City Hall and inside the Department, the Union now forged ahead with its agenda. The pension program was at the top of their list.

Mayor Wagner, remembering the role of the Sanitationmen in getting him reelected, presented to the state legislature a bill which would have

83

given Sanitationmen the option of retiring at 55 or after twenty-five years of service. At that time, they only had the option of retiring at 55 or after thirty years of service.

Both houses of the New York State legislature approved the bill unanimously, but it was vetoed by Governor Rockefeller on February 3, 1962. The Governor was a Republican and very aware of Local 831's role in getting New York City's Democratic mayor reelected.

The Union threatened to strike in protest of the veto.

Despite Wagner's support for the bill, the city warned the Union not to strike. Threatening to invoke the state's Condon-Wadlin law, City Labor Commissioner Harold A. Felix said that a strike would be "not only illegal, but futile." The City made it clear that if the Union did strike, certification as well as dues check-off could be taken away.

In the end, Mayor Wagner personally intervened and met with DeLury. Together, they issued a joint statement expressing "keen disappointment" at the Governor's action and declaring "our goal will be as it has always been in our dealings, to reach an amicable agreement fair to Sanitationmen as well as to the city's interest."

As a result, the Union did not strike, but pressed forward, achieving consistent wage gains, as well as medical coverage and other benefits.

The Union did not let up on their push for a fairer pension and, one year later, in April 1963, Sanmen finally got what they wanted. Governor Rockefeller, voicing some reservations, signed into law a pension bill that allowed Sanmen to retire after 25 years of service at half their final salary.

1965 – The Tipping Point?

An important source of DeLury's power lay in the very nature of the work that Sanmen did. With a mere flourish, DeLury could disperse 10,000 Sanitationmen to carry the union's message throughout a vast city. As the New York Times noted in 1964:

"The members of the sanitation union are unusually effective politically because their days off are rotated so that there are 1,600 men available for canvassing six days every week. Even on official rounds, Sanitationmen have an opportunity for politicking. Where the ordinary politician is barred, they find it easy to stuff mail boxes with campaign literature."

But even with their new-found successes, and a rousing motto of "Go! Go! Go!" – many of the demands of the Union remained pragmatic and, were they accepted, would have profited the Department as well. For example, New York City sanitation trucks, some of them pushing ten years in age, chugged slowly along five-thousand miles of streets. DeLury and the Union applied

USA ARCHIVES

Bobby Kennedy in a guest appearance at the Local 831 Headquarters. He showed up to apologize for referring to Sanmen as "garbagemen."

increasing pressure on the Department to replenish its fleet. The benefit to both the Union and the Department was clear: a happier Sanitationman working in a safer, more comfortable and more productive environment. What might have been construed as a grab for Union power could just as easily been viewed as a potential win-win for both sides.

The Welfare Strike of 1965

In these areas the work of other unions affected Local 831, especially the welfare strike of 1965.

The entire municipal labor movement in New York City sat squarely in the larger picture of the civil rights movement and social change that characterized the '60s. After all, the labor movement was the wellspring for social change and radicalism in America. As has been noted, the phenomenon of the "sit-in," which is often associated with the protest movement of the 1960's, was actually first used as a job action by the Labor movement in the

1930's. But the militancy of the Sixties swept Labor far past mere sit-ins. Strikes became the tactic of choice for Labor activists during this period, and it started with the welfare workers' strike.

NYC welfare workers had begun negotiating a new contract in October, 1964, and after four months of stalemate with the City, went on strike on January 4, 1965.

Their demands contained two special elements.

The first was that Victor Gotbaum's union, DC 37, sought improvements in the welfare system that would benefit welfare recipients. This garnered them the support of civil rights groups. The second was their demand for smaller caseloads. This attracted the attention of other City unions.

If the welfare workers succeeded, it would sound a revolution of sorts. The welfare workers' issue of caseload translated easily to "workload" for Sanitationmen.

But the city immediately responded to the strike by invoking the Condon-Wadlin law and threatening to fire 5,000 welfare workers. Still the welfare workers did not budge: their strike lasted 28 days in an unusually bitter winter that January. Finally the city gave in. Mayor Wagner agreed to stay the workers' dismissal. The welfare workers received salary increases and improved benefits. Most significantly, the City agreed to review the caseloads and hire additional personnel.

It was a win for the welfare workers, and one that every city union shared in.

The welfare strike led to the eventual formation of New York City's Office of Collective Bargaining and the Office of Labor Relations.

The End of the Wagner Years and the Mayoral Election of 1965

Robert Wagner decided not to seek a fourth term in office, citing personal reasons. A friend to both labor as well as to John DeLury, Wagner's departure signaled the end of an era and new times ahead for the Uniformed Sanitationmen's Association.

The Democratic primary was thus opened wide and, among the four candidates, both Abe Beame and Paul Screvane had connections with Local 831 which made them potential favorites of Sanmen.

Beame, a career bureaucrat from Brooklyn and City Comptroller during Wagner's third term, had long aspired to the office of Mayor of New York. Screvane was the former Commissioner of Sanitation and, therefore, was known and liked by many Sanitationmen.

John DeLury praised both, but did not come out for either during the primary race. When Beame won the Democratic nomination, he then received the support of Local 831. Beame declared that he favored an improved pension program for Sanitationmen.

The Republicans put up a relative unknown to New York City politics – John V. Lindsay.

A "Record" for Sanitationmen in 1965

In March 1965, the Sanmen created a new and loud voice for themselves with the publication of the USA Record, their own tabloid. The first issue featured articles on Union negotiations with the city, Sanmen's working conditions, cartoons, and photographs. Other sections were aimed at building morale and a sense of community among the rank and file.

A sampling of titles gives the flavor:

"Which Health Plan Gives The Most? – What GHI Offers"

"Filthy Working Quarters – Millions Available But Not One Cent for Decent Quarters for Sanitationmen"

"The Best Time to Retire"

"Snow! A Sanitationman's Backbreaker!"

"Wage Pact OK'd – Membership's Economic & Political Activity Responsible"

DeLury's Union had political punch and the USA Record gave him a regular and ready outlet for communication. The Record helped him get a grip on that power inside the Union, just as it helped the Union keep a grip on power outside.

DeLury wrote a regular column entitled "Go! Go! Go!" In the August 1965 issue of the Record, just as the Mayoral election was heating up, DeLury wrote:

"Those who aspire to succeed Bob Wagner, must first prove themselves. Nor is it any longer sufficient to point to the label in the lapel, be it Democrat or Republican. Sanitationmen are more sophisticated than that. Sanitationmen are aware that their gains came with both Democrats and Republicans in office. Sanitationmen have not only done well with Wagner – they have also done well with Rockefeller."

Enter John Lindsay

A product of prep school and Yale, John Vliet Lindsay was a man of charm, charisma – and presidential ambitions. He wanted to become Mayor so that, as he put it, "our City can once again be restored as the Empire City of the world."

John Lindsay won the mayoral election and came, as one observer has put it, "not so much to govern, as to rescue the city." Sometimes compared to JFK, tall and handsome, Lindsay held a seat in Congress and, when in New York, surveyed the city from the heights of his base on the Upper East Side.

Perhaps he would have had a happier experience as Mayor if had he heeded certain signs along the way. Such signs included constant requests by Labor leaders, including John DeLury, that Lindsay consult with them. He did not. He rode into town on a high horse as if looking for Camelot, but what he found instead was more like the O.K. Corral.

Chapter Eight

1968 – When a Strike is a Strike

"This is America?"
> - John DeLury as he entered jail for his role in the 1968 Sanitation Strike.

"Call for the National Guard, Mr. Governor."
> - Union consultant Jack Bigel, speaking to Governor Nelson A. Rockefeller and mocking the popular sentiment during the strike.

The mercury moved to just above freezing in the early hours of Friday, February 2, 1968 when Sanitationmen started filling up the park in front of City Hall. Most of the Sanmen had arrived by 7 a.m. The police were there even earlier. John DeLury had called it a "rally." It looked more like a duel at dawn, the City lined up against the Union.

Lindsay Tests Political Muscle of the USA

With 10,000 members in 1968, the Uniformed Sanitationmen's Association weighed in as the smallest of New York City's six major municipal unions. But in terms of political punch, it was second to none. Edward Costikyan, New York County Democratic Chairman, summed it up at the time: "I would today rather have John DeLury's Sanitationmen with me in an election than half the party headquarters in town."

The USA was able to muster and dispatch thousands of members to the right districts when needed. At its Cliff Street headquarters, the USA kept on file over 20,000 index cards showing the place of residence and various political subdivisions of its members, both active and retired. John DeLury's political muscle was taken seriously by Albany. DeLury was not kidding when he said, "Only God can guarantee 100% of the vote... I am sure of 99%."

City Hall nonetheless allowed its contract with the USA to run out in May 1967. By December, the City was still without an agreement with the USA and also bogged down in negotiations with other unions. DeLury and the USA, who had been trying to use productivity as a bargaining chip since 1966, were again beaten back in their efforts to establish Sanmen's "vastly accelerated productivity" to obtain needed wage increases. The City also ignored the Union's attempts to gain greater compensation for job-related injuries which had increased by more than 18% in 1967. At the end of January 1968, John DeLury had few cards left to play: he finally called for a strict adherence to safety rules regulations (translation: 3-day slowdown).

Mayor Lindsay was desperate to demonstrate some mastery of labor relations in time for the next year's mayoral election. In addition, rumors were circulating that the Mayor was a dark horse for the V.P. slot during the 1968 presidential campaign. The looming battle with the Uniformed Sanitationmen's Association provided the opportunity – and perfect timing – for Lindsay to face off with a reputedly tough municipal Union.

A Tale of Two (and then Three) Men

Except for their first names, Lindsay and DeLury had little in common.

Lindsay was a product of the Upper East Side; DeLury grew up in one of Brooklyn's tougher sections, known as "Irishtown." Lindsay stood six feet, four inches; DeLury could match the four inches, but, came up a foot short. Lindsay graduated from Yale; DeLury left high school early in order to go to work. Lindsay was a dreamer; DeLury, a pragmatist. Lindsay was an intellectual and internationalist; DeLury, an Incineratorman of the school who saw all politics, like all garbage, as local. Lindsay was of mythical proportions. DeLury was an ordinary man.

The contest pitting the two seemed like Goliath and David. However, in the largely management-biased news coverage about to unfold, yet another figure came to play a critical role: Governor Nelson A. Rockefeller.

Everything To Lose

As John DeLury well knew, the most powerful weapon in a Union's arsenal is not a strike; it is the threat of a strike. The USA had used that threat often – and effectively.

A history of small, consistent gains made DeLury very confident of his and his Union's ability to negotiate without having to resort to a strike. Progress in the decade since Local 831's birth had been slow, but steady. Unlike other New York City Unions which favored longer-term deals with the City, the USA employed a strategy of going after shorter 12-month contracts.

In this way, the USA mounted a conservative, but nonetheless aggressive, approach to collective bargaining. DeLury did not favor a strike which could

NEW YORK DAILY NEWS

John DeLury has climbed atop a panel truck and asks Sanmen to vote on the contract. The response was a resounding "No," kicking off a 9-day Sanitation Strike on Feb. 2, 1968.

destabilize the solid base, and allow the City an opportunity to use the new Taylor Law that could limit and even turn back some of the Union's gains.

The USA leader also opposed a strike because of timing. DeLury knew better than to strike in February – garbage doesn't smell in the winter. In addition, the recent anti-strike Taylor Law gave the City a great deal of power. The remedies allowed to the City under these new limitations could cripple a Union. For DeLury, another factor weighing against a strike was the question of his own grip on power. DeLury was aware that a strike created a volatile situation in which existing internal Union rifts could deepen and even threaten his own position as president. DeLury had much to lose by a strike.

Mood of the Men

As for the rank and file, although much had been achieved over the past twelve years, their pay and benefits still lagged behind other Unions (notably the police and firemen) , and so they demanded more.

Another problem facing DeLury was a "generation gap" that had developed between older and younger Sanitationmen. A large number of Sanmen had opted to take advantage of the new 20-year pension won by the Union in 1967. These veterans were replaced by a new breed of Sanitationmen that

little-known facts about your well-known

SANITATIONMEN

Dear Neighbors and Friends,

We would like to re-introduce ourselves to you so that we can become better acquainted with you and your problems.

Our object is to give you the service to which you are entitled, within the limits of our duties as your employees. If you have any suggestions which you feel might improve the service and efficiency of our collection, we would be more than pleased to receive them, in writing, and pass them on to our departmental and organizational officials.

Trucks Last Four Years—200,000 Miles

We feel, too, that you might be interested in some **facts** concerning the work we do. For instance, the City has made studies which show that the average heavy-duty collection truck has a productive lifetime of four years and 200,000 miles.

While the City has made a study of the life span of its **machines,** our association of Sanitationmen hired some medical and scientific experts to see how long a Sanitation**man** can work at peak production. The figure is frightening. It is fifteen years!

Old Age Is No Problem

We learned that the mortality of Sanitationmen is age 54. This means that the average Sanitationman will have died eleven years **before** he could obtain any Social Security benefits.

What's the Most Dangerous Job?

Another fact that we discovered through our medical-science study shows that the most dangerous job in America is that of logger-lumberman-woodcutter. The SECOND most hazardous job (because of injuries, accidents, etc.) is that of YOUR own Sanitationman.

had grown up in the relative affluence of the 1950s and 60s. This "green" rank and file were not aware of the Union's accomplishments, and so did not fear for their jobs and pensions as their seniors had done. When City Hall stalled or tried to apply the brakes to contract negotiations, the instinct of these younger rank and file members was to push even harder and faster.

Lindsay, however, wanted nothing to do with labor leaders, equating them with "power brokers." He had made it a campaign promise to resist doing "business as usual" with them. The Mayor relegated what he considered the dirty work of negotiating union contracts to the Office of Labor Relations (OLR) that he had created in 1966. And, in the event that it failed, he had then established the Office of Collective Bargaining (OCB) to take over. DeLury, like several other labor leaders, refused to acknowledge the OCB. Instead, he wanted to deal directly with the Mayor and his staff. But John Lindsay was just not comfortable with blue collar workers." Eric Schmertz, former OCB mediator, described Lindsay as being only "intellectually supportive of unions – the words were there, but the music was not."

The Family Municipal

New York City municipal unions act, in some ways, like a family: what one union gets, another wants. Sanitationmen, of course, knew about the generous wage increase that their union brothers in transit had received from the Mayor just one month earlier. All the Unions were aware of all recent wage settlements, as well as of the City's changing fiscal situation.

As the negotiating arm of City Hall, Herb Haber, Director of the Office of Labor Relations, was overworked. In 1967 alone, he had to negotiate new contracts with four major unions, starting with the second strike of welfare workers, then with the striking teachers, as well as the 90,000 member District Council 37 and the USA.

Adding to Haber's headaches, both the police and firemen threatened to reopen their own contracts for negotiation, if the USA drew any closer to them in wages and benefits. City Hall wanted to set in motion a "whipsawing effect" between rival unions. Haber let it be known that his office would not allow negotiations with the USA to disrupt the "specific relationship of salaries between the uniformed forces."

From their side of the table, Sanitationmen had in their latest contract received only a $450 annual increase compared to the $500 received by the other uniformed services. Sanmen had seen the gap between them and police and firemen get smaller in the previous ten years, but they were still, as always, behind. As a group, the Sanitationmen had long chafed at being "the

LOCAL 831 ARCHIVES
Left: Throughout the 1950s and 1960s, Local 831 used circulars and small booklets like this to educate and inform its rank and file, as well as the City's residents, of matters of concern to the Union and its members.

forgotten men of the city" and, on the occasions when they were noticed, resented being referred to as and treated like "garbagemen." Sanmen had built up a backlog of unrest; a reservoir of anger had risen slowly over the previous decades.

The First Step

Negotiations began in early 1967, but dragged on into the depths of the winter of 1968 before any real movement happened. The Union asked for a $450 annual wage increase; the City countered with $250. An intensive negotiating session ended at 5:00 a.m. on Tuesday, January 30, when the City, with the aid of two mediators, finally offered DeLury a package he felt he could take to his membership: a $400 wage increase, along with a few other improvements to benefits. DeLury tentatively accepted, but he stated clearly that he could not guarantee acceptance by the Union.

The deadlock was never really about money; it was now really about respect. DeLury received his first full dose of this shift in mood at a stewards meeting on Wednesday evening, January 31, 1968. The Union Hall on Cliff Street was filled wall-to-wall with 600 shop stewards. Latecomers waited in the street. DeLury met first with the Union's business agents and then with the negotiating committee. Both groups voted against the City's offer. The USA president presented the offer to the stewards. He was met with loud and angry rumbling. The younger stewards were the most vocal.

Then something happened that caused the younger stewards to quiet down. An older Sanitationman stood up and began to speak about his many years on the job, about how far the Union had come, and how proud he was to count himself a Sanitationman. He ended with this statement: "We may handle garbage, but we aren't garbage!" The men roared approval. Then, an even more senior steward stood up and rather quietly, as if in an intimate conversation with DeLury, matter-of-factly stated, "John, they don't respect us."

The stewards voted unanimously to reject the City's offer.

Unintentionally, Lindsay had succeeded in uniting the two generational factions inside the Union. He had mended a potentially major rift and had instilled all the Sanitationmen with a new solidarity. It remained to be seen, however, whether this would help or hurt DeLury, since his Union was now clearly on a course toward a strike, something the USA president still hoped to avoid.

By refusing to deal directly with DeLury, whose weapon of choice was the threat of a strike, the Mayor had opened himself up to direct attack by the rank and file, who were not trained in the art of "threatening to strike." The only serious weapon they saw in their arsenal was their actual ability to strike. But DeLury was successful in getting them to agree to come for a rally on the grounds of City Hall.

When a Strike is a Strike

The park in front of New York City Hall is miniature in scale, so it didn't take long, on the morning of Friday, February 2, 1968, before it overflowed with 7,000 Sanmen waiting for the rally that John DeLury had called. By itself, the rank and file's boisterous presence was a strong show of strength which might influence negotiations.

The police attempted, with little success, to corral the Sanmen, some of whom had been up through the night and were becoming unruly, into the tight confines of the park. From the very beginning, the meeting displayed the makings of what the New York Times would call a "tumultuous demonstration."

DeLury began punctually at 7 a.m., a symbolic time, as it was the hour most Sanitationmen began their workday. He began, "Now we have a city offer before us for four-hundred dollars," but he did not finish before the heckling and shouts of "Go!" [Union language for "Strike!"] started. He attempted to calm them: "Now wait a minute..." But he was over shouted: "Take the four-hundred and shove it!" "It stinks!" "Tell them to stuff it!" Never one to back down quickly, DeLury tried to reassure the men that negotiations could still work to their advantage. "You must have patience," he urged. "We're going to win this one."

But patience was in short supply. The final straw came when DeLury, trying to prevent an immediate vote, reminded his men that, according to the provisions of the Teamsters' Constitution, there would have to be a vote to strike by mail ballot. That technicality did not purchase DeLury much with the crowd. The men saw it for what it was: a stalling tactic. Some of them were aware that DeLury, in the event of a strike, could be found in violation of the one of the new laws and face jail time. They accused him of being fearful of this: "Why don't you go to jail?" "You're selling us out!" "You're afraid of going to jail!"

No, No, No! – Go, Go, Go!

The shouting and hooting grew in volume. "No contract – no work!" "Let's vote!" Some men started to chant 'Go-Go-Go!" the Union's rallying cry to strike. The rumbling and shouting, turned physical. The men rushed City Hall, surging past the police lines. One contingent headed straight for DeLury and the men around him. He held his position, even as objects started to fly. An egg flew through the air, missing him but striking a reporter.

DeLury got shaken up that morning, but recovered quickly. He then marched straight back into City Hall. Once there, he again met with mediators from the City and waited three hours for John Lindsay to show up for the final showdown.

Despite the raucous scene, New York City Sanitationmen were still

CORBIS

A woman tries to make her way to a mailbox through accumulated garbage during the strike.

technically not striking. DeLury had not yet called for a vote. As long as he was still talking to the Mayor and as long as Sanmen were not striking, it was DeLury's goal to shoot for a contract settlement. He continued to play off the threat of a strike. Lindsay was not biting. Making one last attempt to goad Lindsay into proposing a compromise, DeLury shot high, asking for a $600 annual wage increase. The Mayor: "The request is impossible. We reject it!" In the normal give-and-take of contract negotiations, Lindsay had just been given a prime opportunity to counter with a lesser offer and possibly avoid a strike. The opportunity had been lost.

DeLury marched back to his men. Now fired up, the still spry sixty-three year-old climbed on top of a van, grabbed a bullhorn, and in a taunting voice announced: "The Mayor has turned us down! No contract – no work! He says

'No, no, no!' So we say..." The Sanmen responded on cue with "Go! Go! Go!" This exchange of DeLury's 'No, no, no!' and the Sanmen's 'Go, go, go!" was repeated several more times. Then DeLury, as if he were following strict parliamentary procedure, finally declared, "I accept the motion for go-go-go!" It was unanimous. The New York City Sanitation strike of 1968 had commenced.

DAY ONE
Friday, Feb. 2, 1968
Total Uncollected Garbage at Day's End: 11, 000 tons

In 1968, New York City's population was 7.9 million. Each person generated daily about two and a half pounds of garbage, translating into approximately 10,000 tons (20 million pounds) of garbage to be collected each day. And without the usual mass of Sanmen to remove it, that garbage began to grow...

The City Responds

City Hall counterattacked like lightning. First came a temporary restraining order against the USA, enjoining them against any strike, slowdown or work stoppage. The court scheduled a hearing for Monday to consider the charges. Lindsay also made clear that he would not negotiate with the union so long as the strike was still on. The Mayor suggested to DeLury that it would be nice if, after they had the weekend "off," Sanmen would go back to work on Monday. DeLury's reply: "I don't think so."

"Health Menace?"

With the strike but a few hours old, City Hall raised the specter of rats. Adopting an inflammatory tone designed to turn residents against the strikers, the City summarily announced that rats, roaches and other vermin would soon create a "health menace."

City Hall even fanned public fears of typhoid and other epidemics. To be sure, there would be health concerns if the strike dragged on. Sanitationmen were sensitive to that fact. To its credit, the Union took steps to safeguard the health and safety of certain "special needs" communities of the city. From the beginning of the strike, the USA continued to collect garbage – for no pay – from schools, municipal hospitals, nursing homes and other city facilities.

Mayor Lindsay, in a news conference late Friday afternoon, announced that he considered the sanitation strike "an emergency situation." There was one piece of good news for him. There was no snow in the forecast. Snowfall greatly complicates garbage removal. And, in New York City, Sanitationmen remove the snow. A significant snowstorm would turn the Mayor's bad dream into a nightmare.

DAY TWO
Saturday, Feb. 3, 1968
Total Uncollected Garbage: 22,000 tons

All the Trash That's Printed Doesn't Fit

On Saturday morning, the second day of the strike, newspapers began to weigh in and they turned the situation into a three-ring circus. The smallest ring consisted of pro-strike articles that mentioned the Sanmen's low pay, grievances and poor working conditions.

The next, larger ring was composed of anti-strike articles that focused on the sensational aspects of the strike. Many column inches were devoted to endless descriptions of the garbage littering the streets.

The biggest ring was the editorial pages where the strike got special billing and treatment. Criticism of the labor action by all the major dailies was scathing. There were no real attempts to place the strike in the context of the previous two-hundred year struggle of the American labor movement.

Most vehement in their opposition to the strike was the editorial staff of the New York Times. The strike was less than twelve hours old when the paper hit the streets an editorial titled, "Drowning in Garbage."

NY Times, February 9, 1968
The runaway strike by the city's unionized garbage collectors is the latest miscarriage in a concept of civil service unionism that relies on the illegal application of force to club the community into extortionate wage settlements...

The walkout creates an immediate health emergency that will get worse each day. A heavy snowfall – for which the union openly prays – would turn emergency into disaster. Mayor Lindsay has taken the right and necessary course in moving for an injunction under the state's new Taylor Law. The city cannot surrender to such tyrannical abuse of union power.

Mayor Lindsay immediately adopted the word, "extortionate," and its cousin, "extortion," in his own lashing criticism of the Union and soon adopted the even stronger word, "blackmail", to describe the Sanmen's actions.

The Times editorial accused the U.S.A. membership of being "indoctrinated." This was a highly colored word at that time because it triggered an instant association with another word: communism. There was no budding communist movement inside the Uniformed Sanitationmen's

Association. The main political divides within the Union consisted of Democrats versus Republicans and Yankees versus Mets.

The editors also declared the strike an "immediate health emergency," although an article in a different section of the same edition of the Times quoted Commissioner Edward O'Rourke as saying that any health emergency was "at least several days away."

Also, by calling the strike "illegal," the Times disregarded what many legal experts considered one of the gray areas of the new Taylor law: the "right" of a Union to strike when it is not under contract, which was the situation of the USA at that time.

Other papers carried similar diatribes. To be fair, The Daily News and the New York Post did publish one photograph which showed the Union in a human light. The picture was of three volunteer Sanmen leaving the garage at Delancey Street to collect garbage at schools and hospitals. One Sanman is holding a sign announcing "We're Taking It Away – Without Pay."

There was one newspaper, the Village Voice, that looked at "the other half" of the story and expressed strong support for the striking Sanitationmen. As Sidney Zion noted with sarcasm: "It did not seem to matter to the Mayor and it surely did not concern the public what a sanitation job was worth."

Public Relations vs. Relations with the Public

That Saturday Mayor Lindsay toured Manhattan's West Side; the Bedford-Stuyvesant, Williamsburg and Park Slope sections of Brooklyn; and Long Island City, Queens. Afterwards he described conditions as "serious, but not critical."

Health Commissioner O'Rourke, along for the ride, provided more color: "In four or five days, rats will be getting at the garbage."

Of course, veteran Sanmen were all too familiar with rats. As Sanitationman Tony "Smash" Casalaspro recalls, "In those days you didn't just walk up to a [garbage] can and pick it up. You kicked it first. If it had a lid, first you'd take the lid off, then you kicked it. If there were rats – they'd jump out. Then you pick the can up. Sometimes they were still in there and as you hoisted the can onto the truck, they'd jump out. You'd try to make sure they didn't jump on you."

DAY THREE
Sunday, Feb. 4, 1968
Total Uncollected Garbage: 33,000 tons

Things began to flare up, literally, three days into the strike when street fires began to be set. Most were started for the purpose of burning trash; some were the result of cigarettes and other accidents.

A five alarm fire, causing a house to collapse in Astoria, Queens, had started in a pile of trash on Sunday. Three adjacent houses were damaged and three firemen were injured fighting the fire.

Also, in the small hours of Sunday, someone fired a shot gun blast through the front of a sanitation foreman's house and the next day he received a bomb threat. This incident received major play in the newspapers, stealing front page headlines. The Daily News employed a creative front page layout with a picture of the supervisor in front of the shattered window, while the headlines surrounding him screamed about the heavy casualties in the battle of Khe Sanh. The juxtaposition, at best, was inappropriate. At worst, it was an attempt to imply guilt by association.

Distressed America, Disheveled New York

The New York City Sanitation Strike of 1968 unfolded in the context of a nation that had already become unnerved. February 1968 is remembered as the beginning of the Tet offensive, the bloodiest chapter and turning point in the Vietnam War. At the same time and throughout the nation, much of the promise which the decade had held was not being realized. Labor Unions, in both the private and public sectors, were experiencing greater internal dissent. Personal and financial expectations of workers were starting to be disappointed after decades of post-war affluence for the nation as a whole. New York City, bestrewn with its debris, ablaze with its own refuse, came to symbolize a larger society littered with broken promises and smoldering dreams.

That Sunday, Lindsay finally called and asked DeLury and his advisor, Jack Bigel, to come to Gracie Mansion for a secret meeting. At first they refused, saying that all meetings should be public. In the end, they decided to participate. The Mayor immediately asked how long they expected the strike to last. DeLury told Lindsay that the correct question was not how long, but how much: how much of a wage increase would it take to get the men back to work. The meeting ended in another standoff.

That evening, on his regular Sunday TV program over WNEW, Mayor Lindsay said: "It's a mess all right. We go from crisis to crisis. This one is very, very serious, with all the Sanitationmen not working. It's not yet critical, but it will get there if it continues."

Acting Sanitation Commissioner Maurice Feldman spoke on radio station WNYC that same Sunday evening and fine tuned the Department's advice to city residents, advising everyone that "papers should be tied up in bundles," that garbage cans should only be used for "soggy garbage," and to be sure "to close the lids on garbage cans."

Weekend Warriors – or Scabs?

There was a second secret meeting that Sunday to which the Union was

John DeLury heads to jail to begin a 15-day sentence. To the right can be seen Albert Shanker, President of the United Federation of Teachers, extending a handshake to DeLury along the way.

not invited. This one was between the City and the Governor's office. Lindsay arranged for Deputy Mayor Robert Sweet, and Governor Rockefeller's Executive Secretary, Alton Marshall, to meet with General A.C. "Buzz" O'Hara, the head of the New York National Guard. The object of this meeting was to prepare for the possibility of calling out the Guard in order to break the strike and clean up the mess. The General was not keen on the idea, but half-heartedly agreed to study the logistics of such a mission.

Lindsay took another tour of the streets that Sunday evening. The forecast: only a 10% chance of snow.

DAY FOUR
Monday, Feb. 5, 1968
Total Uncollected Garbage: 43,000 tons

"Don't tell us there's no money. We know how rich this City is... we see it in the garbage every day!" - John DeLury

Garbage, like people, grows in spurts. The biggest spurt takes place over the weekend. Monday is a hard day for Sanitationmen. It is what they call a "heavy load day." That Monday, February 5, 1968, a total of 43,000 tons of accumulated garbage sized up as an especially "heavy-load" day.

"[T]he court has seen fit to find the union in contempt without having heard from the union." - Paul O'Dwyer, Attorney for the USA

That Monday, February 5th, the Union got tossed a different kind of heavy load. The City moved in court to invoke sanctions of the Taylor Act, a new weapon to prevent strikes by public employees. The Taylor Act had replaced the more draconian, and for that reason less practical, Condon-Wadlin Act in 1966. DeLury and Bigel protested that the City was rushing the trial. Despite a brilliant defense by the Union's lawyer, Paul O'Dwyer, at the end of the day Justice Saul S. Streit found DeLury and the Union guilty. The Union was fined heavily and DeLury got two weeks in jail.

Justice Streit, at O'Dwyer's prodding, actually admitted his prejudice against the Sanitationmen before the trial began. O'Dwyer accused him of coming to the conclusion that the Union was guilty before the Union "had opened its mouth." The Judge's response: "You are right about that."

Streit fined the Union $80,000, halted its dues check-off for 18 months, and sentenced John DeLury to 15 days in jail. Paul O'Dwyer commented on the kangaroo court proceedings in a later appeal:

We appeared before the Court in an atmosphere of complete hysteria. Newspapers, radio and television announced to the public that our citizens were about to experience something comparable to the bubonic plague which nearly wiped out London many centuries ago.

As [Health] Commissioner O'Rourke explained later in court, the rats, which had bitten 400 slum-dwelling children last year, might invade the middle class and wealthier sections of our town. While we did not seem to ever get terribly excited while the vermin were attacking the children of the impoverished, our society did get itself in a state of white heat at the thought of rodent escalation.

To top off the impending incarceration of DeLury, Mayor Lindsay that same afternoon held a press conference and announced that he was considering a formal request to Governor Nelson Rockefeller to call out the National Guard "to perform the duties of the Sanitationmen."

An editorial in that morning's Times reinforced the Mayor's position:

It is plain enough that what encourages the garbage noncollectors in their defiant course is confidence that New York is helpless before them – that this greatest of cities must surrender or see itself sink in filth...

> This is not a labor dispute; it is a health emergency. The
> Mayor's necessary course if it persists, is to call on Governor
> Rockefeller for help in establishing an emergency garbage-
> removal service.

The fact that the editorial was published several hours before the Mayor's
press conference led the Sanitation Union to believe that the Times' editorial
staff had collaborated with the Mayor and his aides in an effort to shape
public opinion.

The weather forecast that Monday evening was for continued cold, with
no snow in sight.

DAY FIVE
Tuesday, Feb. 6, 1968
Total Uncollected Garbage: 53,000 tons

On Tuesday, Paul O'Dwyer, who had asked for a stay of execution of the
15-day jail sentence for John DeLury, made final arguments before Justice
Streit. The Court would not budge, and DeLury was ordered to jail the next
day.

Negotiations between the City's mediators and the U.S.A. finally resumed
Tuesday afternoon. DeLury attended. When asked by reporters how he
thought his imprisonment would effect continuing negotiations, he answered
that it would go more slowly, but that he would be in twice-daily contact with
the Union's team: "They can negotiate. I've got to approve it."

At this point, nearly two days had been wasted in court. The city's first
mistake lay in calling what they thought was the Union's bluff of a strike.
The second was in expecting the strike to last only a couple of days, as had
the two-day strike of 1960. Now these mistakes were greatly compounded by
jailing DeLury.

Mayor Lindsay was clearly playing to the public and trying to look tough
to the City's other unions. A few years earlier, Mayor Wagner had carefully
avoided even using the word "strike" and had helped bring a quick end to the
1960 "stoppage." In contrast, Lindsay moved to raise the stakes by arming
himself with the Taylor Law and stepping further back onto what he saw as
the moral high ground.

This, despite the fact that the Union had even agreed to increase the
number of volunteer Sanmen removing garbage and refuse from hospitals,
schools and other "emergency facilities." There were now five hundred
Sanitationmen performing this work for no pay.

Rockefeller, also seen as a potential presidential candidate, tried to
outflank the Mayor. Late Tuesday, the Governor responded to Mayor Lindsay's
request for mobilization of the National Guard. Rockefeller announced that,
in order for him to approve that action, the Mayor would "have to say he's

Mayor Lindsay toured the streets regularly during the strike, always accompanied by a retinue of reporters and photographers.

lost control and ask the state to come in."

Rockefeller, an astute politician, had placed Lindsay in a no-win situation. He knew that the Mayor would not want to publicly admit his inability to govern the City. Rockefeller was hoping that Lindsay would yield to the Union. The Governor, as he admitted later that week, did not feel that the Union's wage demands were unreasonable.

The Governor's non-committal response to the Mayor's feeler for backup from the National Guard was a strong indicator of troubles to come.

The Tuesday evening weather forecast predicted only a 10% probability of snow.

DAY SIX
Wednesday, Feb. 7, 1968
Total Uncollected Garbage: 63,000 tons

Except for the garbage, everything was in motion on Wednesday, the sixth day of the strike. John DeLury was headed to jail, John Lindsay flew back and forth to Albany, USA headquarters had become Strike Central, and City Hall played revolving door to dozens of the City's labor leaders as the Mayor sought to persuade other Unions to support his stand against the Sanmen.

But, the most closely watched movement of the day belonged to nature: a snowstorm over the Midwest aiming, it seemed, straight for The Big Apple.

That morning, DeLury packed his toothbrush, a few books and was driven in a black sedan to the Civil Jail, a red brick building at 434 West 37th Street. Awaiting him was a four-piece band, more than 200 Sanitationmen cheering their support, and a labor contingent that included two of the most powerful Union heads in New York City, Albert Shanker, President of the United Teachers Federation, and Victor Gotbaum, Executive Director of DC 37.

In an interview that John Lindsay gave in 1975, he stated that DeLury was anxious to go to jail and asked the Mayor to ensure that he would be the only Sanitation Union leader to do jail time, in order to become a "martyr." Based on interviews with people who knew and worked with DeLury, he was not anxious to go to jail. There was, however, little alternative and he knew it. The Taylor Law was clear: as leader of a striking municipal union, DeLury could be sentenced to 30 days in jail.

Lindsay Invites Rockefeller to Join the Fray

On that Wednesday, Feb. 7, 1968, John Lindsay was headed upriver. That was the day for his regularly scheduled trip to Albany for his annual appeal for funds before the Legislature's Finance Committee. The trip also provided him with an opportunity to meet face-to-face with the Governor to discuss the sanitation strike.

Over breakfast with the Mayor, the Governor stood firm on the point that

Lindsay found most irksome: that the Mayor would have to admit that "he had lost control" before Rockefeller would consider a request to call out the Guard. By the end of breakfast, however, Lindsay and his aides believed that when push came to shove, the Governor would ultimately support the Mayor.

Later that morning, Lindsay made a "hurried helicopter trip" back to New York City and, upon arrival, called a meeting of the City's labor leaders. The first man he called upon was Victor Gotbaum, one of the few union heads with whom he enjoyed good relations.

The Mayor asked Gotbaum, whose DC 37 included municipal workers ranging from Parks Department employees to city laborers, to take over the sanitation duties and clean up the streets. Despite their friendship and the Mayor's influence over DC 37's own contract that was soon due for renewal, Gotbaum did not take long to respond: "Management had a right to ask, and I had a right to say 'No.'"

Other city labor leaders displayed the same solidarity with the striking Sanitationmen. This was a major victory for the Union. If Gotbaum, as head of one of the largest municipal unions, or any several of them together had acquiesced to the Mayor's request, it would probably have broken the strike. Gotbaum's was an act of union solidarity that Local 831 would never forget.

The Battle for Public Opinion

Sanitationmen were winning on the labor front; however, on the public relations front, they were getting murdered. All the major daily newspapers opposed the strike. They portrayed it as a standoff between the Union and the City. Each was waiting for the other to blink first. The U.S.A. hoped the public would quickly tire of the nuisance of uncollected garbage, while the Mayor and his aides counted on public support to rein in a "runaway" strike.

With DeLury in jail, the Union was represented by a 70-man negotiating committee, together with the Union executive officers. Finally, of course, there were the 600 shop stewards. DeLury handed responsibility for direct contact with the Mayor to Jack Bigel, Al Katz and Paul O'Dwyer.

Bigel, more than anyone, stepped up to the plate. One of the foremost unionists and labor leaders of New York City since the 1930s, Bigel was the architect of much of the successful negotiating and political strategy employed by the Uniformed Sanitationmen's Association. He was the U.S.A.'s point man, the go-to guy. If the going got rough, he could play the hatchet man. Bigel combined a ferocity of intellect and a physical presence that allowed him to dominate most opponents.

So it happened that Bigel was facing off with the City when a forecaster for the United States Weather Bureau spoke the words that so many in the City were dreading: a "severe winter storm," was approaching and would bring four or more inches of snow. This is what the striking Sanmen were hoping for, believing that the City would now be forced, as DeLury put it, "to get off the dime" and make a decent offer. They saw the threat of snow as icing on the cake. Mayor Lindsay saw it as the final straw.

Lindsay reacted quickly and decisively, laying down an ultimatum for Sanmen to return to work by 7:00 a.m. the next morning. If they did not, Lindsay threatened to "ask Governor Rockefeller to make available those forms of state assistance I believe vital to the protection of our citizens from disease, fire, or vermin."

Negotiations between Bigel and Herb Haber, Director of the City's Office of Labor Relations, continued throughout Wednesday night and blurred on into Thursday morning, before they finally ended at 6:30 a.m. Still, no agreement.

DAY SEVEN
Thursday, Feb. 8, 1968
Total Uncollected Garbage: 73,000 tons

In Bondage and Beset by Rats?

Rats, at least the City-made version, continued to loom large. Mayor Lindsay met and posed with the Board of Health, which announced the first health emergency in New York City since 1931. With the Health Emergency in place, Lindsay then ordered 3,000 truck drivers and laborers in eight separate city departments to pick up garbage and assume the duties of the Sanitationmen. But the order was not executed, since not one department could find workers willing to cross the strike line. It was a total refusal, the same as he had received from his friend, DC 37 Executive Director Victor Gotbaum.

On Thursday morning, Gotbaum announced that "if the city forces any member of Council 37 to do out-of-title scab work, then Council 37 will call a strike of the affected workers." Gotbaum also warned that any attempt to penalize workers for refusing the sanitation detail would result in his calling a strike. No small threat coming from a man who controlled 90,000 municipal workers.

Some labor leaders were surprised at the Mayor's attempt to switch workers to the Sanitation Department, but others suspected the Mayor of attempting to "set the stage" for his request to the Governor for mobilization of the Guard. These suspicions were reinforced when Lindsay held an impromptu press conference that day at 8:15 a.m. where he said

At some time, some place, all citizens of New York City reach a point beyond which they refuse to be pushed. In that crisis, they find their ultimate level of resistance... Now is the time, and here is the place, for the city to determine what it is made of; whether it will bow to unlawful force or whether it will resist

with all the strength and courage that eight million people can find within themselves...

Because of this grave emergency, I said in a letter to the Governor, I respectfully request that you provide whatever assistance may be available under the law, including use of the organized militia, if necessary... In plainer language, that means the possible use of the New York State National Guard. I have made this request only after serious deliberation and a full awareness of the opposition it will face. The condition of New York City, however, is desperate. Firm, decisive action is needed to prevent desperation from degenerating into disaster.

Fifty-five minutes later that Thursday morning, Lindsay was having breakfast for the second day in a row with Rockefeller. Because of all the public support, reinforced by the Health Emergency, the overall worsening situation, the strong support from the city's press, and the latest refusal by municipal workers to take over Sanmen's duties, Lindsay assumed that the Governor would now give him a positive response to his request for the Guard.

But the Governor disappointed him. Rockefeller saw a chance to insert himself directly into the situation, and took it. He did not refuse Lindsay's request; instead, he cagily requested the Mayor's permission to "study the situation" more closely. Mayor Lindsay had no choice but to agree.

"A Rockefeller Production"

First, the Governor assembled the players and his own team, including Victor Borella, who had handled labor relations for the Rockefellers and had even helped the family form its own "private union" for the construction of Rockefeller Center. Next, Rockefeller convinced Lindsay to let DeLury out of jail for the day. Then he invited a half-dozen of the city's major labor leaders to join him at the Governor's offices that afternoon.

Rockefeller set it up so that all communication between the City and the Union be routed through himself and his staff, primarily Vincent McDonnell, chairman of the State Mediation Board; Alton Marshall, his chief of staff, and, of course, Borella.

Rockefeller's chummy, back-slapping approach to the city's labor leaders stood in contrast to Lindsay's formality and aloofness that he displayed toward these same men. The Governor was on a first-name basis with many, including John DeLury. They knew each other well and, in fact, Rockefeller had gone out of his way to engage the Sanitation Union President. "Rocky" was a frequent guest at testimonials and birthday parties for DeLury.

The Governor played the perfect host and arranged for an unending train

NEW YORK DAILY NEWS

John DeLury leaves jail, cheered by Sanmen.

of food. DeLury, after dining on a spread that included steak sandwiches, french fries, salad and apple pie, quipped to the press that it was "the best meal I had since I went to jail."

The cozy and congenial atmosphere created by the Governor made a favorable impression on the Union, but it made Lindsay and his staff increasingly uncomfortable. Nonetheless, Rockefeller met with Lindsay and persuaded him to agree to an expanded mediation panel in order to break the current impasse.

The two original mediators, Arvid Anderson and Walter Eisenberg, were now joined by three new members, one each appointed by the Governor; the Mayor; and the Uniformed Sanitationmen's Association. The Governor chose Vincent McDonnell and Mayor Lindsay picked Jesse Friedin, a lawyer and member of the Board of Collective Bargaining. The Union selected Lester Connell, who was secretary-treasurer of Teamsters Joint Council 16.

Some members of Mayor Lindsay's team were suspicious of the Governor's motives. They were upset and frustrated at having been kept in the dark about the overall progress of the negotiations and felt that the Mayor had, in essence, retreated from the tough stance he had declared at his press conference that same morning. The Governor had seized the political initiative.

The Mayor arrived home at Gracie Mansion just in time to see himself get sucker-punched by the Governor on the six o'clock news. In a statement "conveniently timed for the convenience of live television coverage," Rockefeller said, "I'm encouraged by events during the course of the day."

Sanmen respond to the Mayor's accusations describing them as 'vociferous' and 'black-mailers'.

The Governor had purposely not invited Lindsay to be part of this major televised address to the city. He made it plain that it was he who was most capable of the "decisive action" that Lindsay had said was needed. The end of his speech made it seem that the other parties were subservient to his command: "The Mayor and the Union have agreed to this course of action. The panel is now at work." For Lindsay, it was a smack in the face.

Lindsay was further battered by some of the labor leaders Rockefeller had asked to weigh in on the strike. Victor Gotbaum had not only shut out the possibility of DC 37 members being used to scab, but had threatened the possibility of a general strike if the Guard was brought in. On the same note, Morris Iushewitz, secretary of the New York City Central Labor Council, AFL-CIO, commented on the Guard: "It would be union-busting of the worst sort. It would be catastrophic in the long range for both the City and the Unions." Iushewitz pointed to negotiations, not troops, as the solution.

The panel of five mediators finally got to work early Thursday evening. They had been given only until midnight to issue a report. As mediators, they could not impose the terms of a settlement; they could only recommend them.

For its part, the USA's 400 shop stewards waited through the night, ready to vote on the panel's recommendations the moment they arrived. Sanitationmen were anxious to return to work, having already lost a full week's pay. The Union was ready to accept any reasonable offer over the $400.

The mediation panel listened, first, to the city, represented by OLR Director Haber and Deputy Director Bill Hediger, and then to the Union, represented by DeLury, O'Dwyer and Bigel. The panel then retired to discuss it among themselves. Vincent McDonnell, chair of the State Mediation Board, was the first to be convinced that settlement by mediation "was far preferable to mobilizing the Guard, a course of action he saw as potentially disastrous."

The panel also asked how the National Guardsmen, without any training, were going to take over the duties of the city's Sanitationmen and deal with 80,000 tons of trash on the streets, not to mention the continuing daily load of 10,000 tons?

It was still not snowing.

DAY EIGHT
Friday, Feb. 9, 1968
Total Uncollected Garbage: 83,000 tons

At 2:42 a.m. Friday morning, the mediators submitted their recommendation. The panel suggested a $425 wage increase and a 12-month contract. In addition, they backed the Union's requests for double time pay for Sunday work, and a differential of five percent for night shifts. No improvements to the pension program were included.

The first reaction of the Union leaders was negative. DeLury and Bigel had hoped for at least another two and a half percent contribution from the city toward pensions. The two Union leaders met in private and after a short discussion, they emerged to say they had decided to recommend acceptance of the offer. They were careful to note that the recommendation was subject to approval by the stewards, who were standing by to vote immediately.

The $425 did not represent much of an increase over what the city had offered before the strike. To be exact, it was only $25 more per year. DeLury and Bigel were going back almost empty handed, except for the double time and night differential. They knew, however, that the Sanitationmen were ready to go back to work. Besides, the Union president and his chief advisor were pragmatists and knew the union would live to fight for pensions again another day, or at least in the next round of contract negotiations. At this point in the strike, DeLury and Bigel were finally willing to call it a draw.

Principles, or Politics?

John Lindsay, however, was sticking to his guns. Forty-two minutes after the Union accepted the mediators' proposal, the Mayor rejected it, arguing that it was a matter of principle.

Governor Rockefeller, informed of the Mayor's rejection of the McDonnell panel's decision, said: "I am very sorry to hear that" and, at 3:40 a.m. that Friday, went home to sleep. The Mayor was making the miniscule amount of one and one-quarter cents per hour a major stumbling block.

The strike, which should have been over, had now found new life. Across town at Union headquarters, DeLury, O'Dwyer and Bigel informed the 400 shop stewards of the mediators' proposal. They were jubilant for a few minutes until they were told of Lindsay's rejection. Nonetheless, the stewards voted in favor of it as a show of their willingness to end the strike. Their vote to accept, in the face of the Mayor's decision to reject it, was a symbolic gesture, but one designed to improve their standing in the public's eye. Now the Union had to get ready for the next round. A Union steward complained, "Lindsay just wouldn't let Rocky get credit for settling the strike – the contract is a political football that's just getting kicked around."

A little after 4:00 a.m. that Friday morning, and not much more than an hour after the mediators had made their recommendations, Mayor Lindsay held a press conference at Gracie Mansion. He emphasized that the additional annual pay increase for Sanmen would upset relationships with other unions and make it impossible to establish "sensible, coherent labor relations in the future."

When a reporter asked him what should be done, the Mayor answered:

I said yesterday the city would not pay blackmail in order to conclude this strike. The proposed settlement, in my view, asks the city to pay a little blackmail... Nothing is left to do but have the National Guard come in. Mediation has been tried and failed.

In the meantime that Friday morning, the strike was moving into its eighth day and John DeLury was headed back to jail.

Playing Soldiers?

The Governor and Bob Sweet, the Deputy Mayor, discussed possible alternatives over breakfast. Sweet insisted that the city would accept a settlement only if it was based on a process of fact-finding or arbitration and only after the strike had been called off.

After the unproductive meeting with Sweet, the Governor tried to call the Mayor to ask him to reconsider his rejection of the mediators' proposal, but Lindsay was out touring the streets. When reporters informed him of the telephone call, he responded: "There is nothing to reconsider. We'll live with this and fight as long as we can."

Besides the support of the press, Mayor Lindsay was encouraged by the response of the city's residents. That Friday more than 1,800 citizens, three times more than on the preceding days, telephoned the Governor's office. The majority of them urged the Governor to call out the Guard.

Labor leaders, of course, responded quite differently. Morris Iushewitz stepped up his criticism of the Mayor calling him "a boy who wanted to play with soldiers like a kid."

Solidarity with "the Privates"

Of immediate concern to the Mayor was the possible threat of a general strike in sympathy with the Sanitationmen. This threat was again leveled at the city that Friday by other unions, including the Social Service Employees' Union, expressing solidarity with the Sanmen.

Even more alarming to the Mayor and his staff, certain private-sector unions were now calling for a sympathy strike if troops were mobilized. These included the powerful International Ladies Garment Workers Union (ILGWU) and, significantly, Local 813, a Teamsters' union whose workers were responsible for private collection of refuse from hotels, restaurants, and other businesses in the city. If commercial garbage, usually collected by these "privates," were added to the nearly 90,000 tons of refuse already on the street, the city would truly choke on its own waste.

A steady stream of labor leaders continued to lobby the Governor. With John DeLury once again in jail, Jack Bigel represented the USA. The USA was greatly encouraged and strengthened by the support of the city's other unions. The threat to call in the Guard had galvanized them in opposition to the city. A statement by Harry Van Arsdale, Jr., President of the New York City Central Labor Council, reflects their strong support: "We will not tolerate the use of militia against any workers." A general strike by his Council's 1.2 million rank-and-file would involve saleswomen, clerks, welfare workers, newspapers and transport workers. A sympathy strike of that magnitude would have paralyzed New York.

The Governor was not yet willing, however, to drop his option of mobilizing the National Guard. This threat was his primary leverage over both the union and, just as importantly, the Mayor. That Friday he again timed his appearance for the evening television news broadcast, and announced, "I can call out the National Guard and, if necessary, I will."

Shortly after his television appearance, the Governor called Lindsay to urge that they meet in private that evening. But Lindsay was not willing to meet personally. The New York Daily News hit the target when they reported that the Governor and Mayor had reached agreement in one area: "...they'd like to bury each other. In garbage."

Lindsay did, however, send his most trusted aide, Robert Sweet, who met with Rockefeller's lead man, Alton Marshall. Later that evening they were joined by the Governor and Attorney General Louis Lefkowitz. On the union side, Bigel and other labor representatives including Joe Trerotola, the president of Teamsters Joint Council 16, met with Vincent McDonnell and the Governor's labor advisor, Victor Borella. Trerotola, whose Teamsters members controlled most commercial trucking into the city, told the Governor bluntly: "If you bring the Guard in, we'll shut this city down so tight a baby won't be able to get a bottle of milk."

Meanwhile, the Governor's office had decided that binding arbitration was the most attractive solution. Binding arbitration meant that whatever the arbitrator determined must be accepted by both parties. Neither the City nor the Union liked arbitration, but both had come to the point of agreeing to it in principle.

The bargaining broke down, however, during attempts to agree on the "base" of the contract settlement. Bob Sweet held to the Mayor's position that the City would not agree to an arbitration settlement that awarded the Union more than the City's previous offer of a $400 increase. These terms were unacceptable to the USA: they could not go back to the men with the same or fewer dollars than they had refused before the strike. All discussions ended just before dawn on Saturday, February 10.

Rockefeller finally concluded that arbitration was not going to work, and at the same time opposition to calling out the Guard was growing. So, he decided that he, the Governor, might need to take absolute control.

That Friday evening Rockefeller called his counsel, Bob Douglass, in Albany, and delivered the following drastic order: "I'll be up Sunday night, and I want a bill ready authorizing the state to take over sanitation in New York City. Use the Public Health Law. Use anything. Just get it done." The Governor planned to take control of the New York City Sanitation Department.

Douglass set to work frantically to try to get the legislation ready for Monday.

Still, no snow.

DAY NINE
Saturday, Feb. 10, 1968
Total Uncollected Garbage: 93,000 tons

On Saturday, February 10th, John Lindsay yet again received strong support from the press for his hard-line stance. The New York Daily News applauded the Mayor's "refusing to bow before money-grabbing demands of Sanitation Workers, even after Governor Nelson A. Rockefeller gave his Honor's arm a twist... Instead of backing the Mayor by calling up national guardsmen to show sanitation Union head John DeLury who was boss, the Rock tried to harvest some political hay..."

The Times echoed the Daily News, but recognized the impasse:

The dismal reality of the situation created by the Governor's endorsement of the liberalized mediation proposal is that he

Right: John DeLury poses against backdrop of garbage in 1968.

cannot now mobilize the Guard without virtually insuring a general strike by all municipal civil service employees and perhaps by all New York labor.

The Times portrayed Lindsay as the hero, the Union as the villain, and Rockefeller as the crooked conspiring banker. Meanwhile, Rockefeller spent Saturday continuing to listen to various labor leaders vividly portray the consequences if the Guard were called out to deal with what would become a general strike. Rockefeller was forced to confront the possibility of a blood-stained ending to the strike. Finally, with a trembling voice and tears in his eyes, he responded to Bigel and the other Union men in the room:

I know what the National Guard means. I know personally. The National Guard was used to break a strike in which a family corporation was involved when I was a child. Men and women were killed. The consequences of military force are terrible. I cannot inflict that upon a city already wracked with problems. I will not use the National Guard. There must be another way. We will find that way. But under no circumstances, and irrespective of the political consequences to me, will I use the National Guard.

The incident which stirred these strong emotions in Rockefeller was the Ludlow Massacre, which took place in Ludlow, Colorado in 1914. A group of mine workers were striking the Colorado Fuel and Iron Company when the owner of the mine, John D. Rockefeller, arranged for the Colorado governor to call in the National Guard. The miners and their families were huddled in tents when the militia opened fire. Over 60 strikers and members of their families were shot dead or burned alive in their tents when the camp was set ablaze by the troops.

Besides this historical reason, Rockefeller was also simply not willing to destroy his good relations with labor for the sake of his rival, John Lindsay.

The Strike Ends

Finally, the Governor made his move: he asked the USA to tell the men to go back to work. In return, he promised to put the Sanitation Department under the emergency authority of the state and, until a permanent settlement was worked out, he guaranteed that the state would pay the Sanitationmen the extra $250,000 recommended by the mediators. The Union leaders accepted the Governor's terms on a handshake. The strike was over.

In a 6:00 p.m. televised announcement, the Governor explained that not calling out the National Guard was the most important and crucial decision he had made since he became Governor. He described the logistical and

News conference following the settlement of the strike through arbitration. From left, Jack Bigel, John DeLury and publicist Howard Rubenstein.

financial factors that made that step impossible.

He further pointed out that the Guard was totally untrained and unprepared to take over the functions of the Union. As to dollars, the Governor projected that for one 60-day period alone, the Guard would cost the city $15 million, as opposed to the $250,000 that it would take to solve the problem for the Sanitationmen for the current year.

He then stated that "sanitation work is far more dangerous and difficult than the people generally realize, and I'd like to say to you that the 10,000 men in the Sanitation Department average 3,600 accidents a year, and they're veterans and they're trained." It was a small tip of the hat, but one most welcome by the Sanitationmen.

Finally, the Governor announced his proposal for the state to take over responsibility of the Sanitation Department:

I will ask the Legislature in a special message on Monday, when they will be convened, to authorize the State to take over the responsibility for the Sanitation Department's functions – men and equipment. We will do that as soon as this authorization has been granted and the men will be paid at the rate which the mediation panel recommended – $425 over their present wage scale.

117

And now, to conclude this statement, I'd like to give you some good news. I have talked to the union, I have asked them to go back to work immediately. They have agreed to do so, and the men will start back this evening, or late tonight.

One could almost hear a collective cheer go up throughout the City. Meanwhile, back at Gracie Mansion, the Mayor had not been briefed in advance about the Governor's planned television appearance, receiving a telephone call to that effect only minutes before. The Mayor was outraged. He and his aides made arrangements for an immediate radio broadcast of a brief statement in response to Rockefeller.

I am shocked that Governor Rockefeller has capitulated to the union that is striking unlawfully against eight million New Yorkers. This strike was called in defiance of a state law sponsored and signed by Governor Rockefeller himself.

The Mayor promised a full report by the next day and the majority of the public were jubilant that the strike was finally over.

But everyone's attention was riveted on the logistics of removing 100,000 tons of garbage from the streets, a feat of Herculean magnitude.

The Tide Turns

While the city cheered their Mayor, support for the legislation that Rockefeller promised the USA grew weaker. In fact, it would never develop. The next day, Sunday, state legislators were hit with a barrage of letters and phone calls supporting Mayor Lindsay. By Wednesday, February 14, it was clear that the Governor would not be granted the emergency powers which he had requested in order to take over the Sanitation Department of New York City.

So, the ball was thrown back to binding arbitration. Finally, on February 29, 1968, the City and the USA agreed to a pay increase of $425, retroactive to January 1, 1968. The award package also included a 2.5% increase in the city's pension contribution and double time pay for Sunday work.

The USA Seizes the Initiative

Sanitationmen came away from the strike with only an additional fifty cents a week, as well as a few improvements in benefits. It was very little more than they had been offered before the nine day strike. They also walked away with a bloody nose in terms of their relationship with the city.

John DeLury was out of jail. But it was while he was in jail that he made what might have been the most important phone call during the strike – to a brilliant young publicist named Howard Rubenstein. In the aftermath of the strike, Rubenstein mounted a ferocious public relations campaign aimed at finally presenting the Sanmen's side of the strike. It was timely. Except for the Village Voice, which called John DeLury "probably the most responsible labor leader in town," it was clear that the newspapers were still strongly aligned with the Mayor.

The USA, therefore, sought out radio and television to get its message out. The public now got to hear labor's version, "the other half" of the story. Television was the ideal medium for depicting the graphic pictures of the inhuman conditions that made up the life of a Sanitationman. Rats, not just in the garbage, but in the garages and lunchroom "facilities" of the Sanitation Department. Broken equipment, held together with a combination of spot welds and bubblegum. Trucks often lacked heat; rusted holes were stuffed with rags and newspapers to try to keep out deadly carbon monoxide. And with more and more horrific images, the television cameras told the story of a living hell.

This campaign by DeLury and the USA signaled the beginning of a new attitude by the city toward Sanitationmen. It did not mark the end of the underappreciated and maligned worker deprecatingly known as the "garbage man," but it was the beginning of the end.

DeLury and the USA were able to use their new-found voice in the media to continue their oldest of battles. This slow growth of public appreciation for the work of the Sanitationmen was the great victory of the USA's strike. It was the fight for the most basic need of every worker and human being. It was the fight for respect and dignity.

USA record
Uniformed Sanitationmen's Association

VOL. VI, NO. 1   OCTOBER 1970

WE ROLL WITH ROCK

Governor "Proud" Of Our Support

GO...GO...GO!

The Sanitation Union's endorsement of Governor Rockefeller for re-election brought a strong response from New York's chief executive.

In a statement at a crowded press conference in the Governor's office, Mr. Rockefeller said:

I am proud of this endorsement. It comes from men who perform hard work.

It comes from men who perform hazardous work.

It comes from men who perform indispensable work.

Today, everybody talks about the environment—a cleaner world, a more wholesome world.

And I'll tell you where that kind of world begins. It starts with sanitationmen.

They are the front-line troops in the struggle for a cleaner world. They are street environmentalists, every one of them.

They do something about the environment every day in this city.

I am grateful for the endorse-

(continued on page 5, col. 3)

UNION READIES CONTRACT TALKS

One day after the Union's negotiating committee finished an all day session to adopt a wage program for the imminent negotiations, Mayor Lindsay announced that the city is in another seasonal money jam requiring an immediate job freeze and projected the possibility of "pay-less" pay days.

Preceding this latest Lindsay gloom-cast were similar prophecies by labor relations director Herbert Haber that the city faced bankruptcy if it would have to meet the demands of the unions representing the uniformed forces, among them the Uniformed Sanitationmen's Association.

In its session the committee was warned that as the union goes further down the road in November and December, the gloom will become even thicker and the predictions more disastrous.

Although the city is perenially short of money, undoubtedly the administration's immediate goals are to shoot down wage demands and create an atmosphere of public support for hold-the-line policies.

It was pointed out in the committee discussion that City Hall will have some short-term success in winning the facade of public support. Almost immediately, it can now be predicted, can we expect to see editorial support of the city posture and blasts against the wage demands of the Sanitationmen's union.

(continued on page 2)

Local 831 backed Governor Rockefeller in his successful bid for re-election in 1970. It also backed Mayor John Lindsay's successful re-election in 1971. After the Strike of 1968, the Mayor had become very supportive of the Union.

Chapter Nine

Wildcat!

Definition of wildcat:

1) Any of various wild felines of small to medium size, including the bobcat.
2) An oilwell drilled in an area not known to be productive.
3) A quick-tempered person.
4) A person regarded as fierce.
5) A workers' action unauthorized by the officials of their union.

In early July 1975, in response to sudden layoffs, a 3-day wildcat erupted. The action was not organized by the Union or calculated by any cabal. Rather, it was sparked by a handful of rank and file members expressing their frustration with the sudden layoff of thousands of Sanitation Workers by the City. That frustration soon exploded into a full-blown action. This chapter is about that action and how the fate of the Uniformed Sanitationmen's Association was affected by what would become known as the New York City Fiscal Crisis of the mid-1970s. The wildcat action – though initially successful – marked the beginning of a long stretch of dark years for the Sanitationmen. In the first two years alone, 50,000 city workers were laid off, a two-year wage deferral was imposed and a slew of other givebacks were crammed down the throats of municipal employees, uniformed forces included. To top it off, John DeLury's health was failing. It was at this moment of crisis that a new generation of leadership started to take shape.

"By the way, there'll be no white elephants rolling in the city tomorrow. You can take that to the bank!"
- Shop Steward and wildcatter John O'Keefe, announcing

■ Wildcat!

DAILY NEWS
NEW YORK'S PICTURE NEWSPAPER®

FINAL ★★★★

15¢

Vol. 57. No. 109   New York, N.Y. 10017, Thursday, October 30, 1975   Sunny, cool, 47-55. Details p. 135

FORD TO CITY: DROP DEAD

Vows He'll Veto Any Bail-Out

Abe, Carey Rip Stand

Stocks Skid, Dow Down 12

Three pages of stories begin on page 3: full text of Ford's speech on page 36

NEW YORK DAILY NEWS

President Gerald Ford was not only indifferent to NYC's plea for help, but also picked on the supposedly high pay of Sanmen as a major factor in causing the City's fiscal woes.

that no san trucks would be operating during the wildcat.

Monday, the "heavy-load day," was always rough on Sanmen. Weekends produced garbage; likewise, and like always, Sanmen – especially on Mondays – had to produce. Long after Local 831 had won the forty-hour week in 1956,

122

the Department still required the men work a ten-hour day on Mondays.

Monday, June 30, 1975, was especially difficult for young Sanitationman Harry Nespoli, but for a different reason. He had worked his usual route in Districts 32 and 34 in Manhattan on that early summer day, with temperatures hitting the low eighties, the heat adding to the grind – and the smell – of the day's workload. But it had already started to cool as Nespoli drove back to his "home garage" in Brooklyn District 6. The 30-year old Sanman was looking forward to cooling off and relaxing when arrived home, maybe take in a Yankees game on the tube that evening.

Nespoli did not watch baseball that night. In fact, he never made it home that day, or for the next two days. A different kind of heavy load awaited him that Monday when he walked into his garage. Everywhere Sanmen were buzzing like hornets, every telephone was tied up and a long teletype was still clacking its way in from Department headquarters. The teletype spewed out onto the floor a yard-long piece of paper with the names of 2,934 sanmen – Nespoli's among them – who were told that they were laid off, effective immediately. Although the City had been pleading poverty and threatening massive layoffs for over one year, Nespoli could not believe his eyes. He asked a couple of guys for a push to get his banged-up VW Bug started, then drove straight to Local 831's downtown headquarters on Cliff Street where a senior Union official advised him: "Kid, go find another job."

Nespoli was not interested in another job. He wanted the job that had been his one hour earlier, a job that had been his for the last five years, a job he had grown to like. Nespoli – a former running back who had been signed by the Jets farm team – had recently resurrected the Sanitation football team, naming it "New York's Strongest." Nespoli had felt secure in his vocation of Sanman.

I'm thinking it ain't real. I just bought a house. This is a city job. What layoff? The official notice said it was not because of work performance, but because...

Rejecting the option of thirty-two weeks of unemployment checks offered by the City, but at the same time needing to take action, Nespoli brought the situation to the men in his District. That was all that was needed, for the men took it from there. As Nespoli later described it:

District 6 had a reputation as a "rebel district" inside the Department.
Some guys used telephone poles to barricade the garage doors... and suddenly, a lot of trucks developed flat tires... Then there was the organizing of the picket lines – 24 hours round the clock. Senior men picketed during the day. You expect them to do the bastard shift? So then after Six was secured, some guys parked their asses outside the dumps. The dumps are locked

– nobody's going anywhere.

If only District 6 in Brooklyn was involved, the action probably would have failed. But, in order to fulfill his extra-curricular football activities, Nespoli had been assigned to work in Districts 33 and 34 in Manhattan. As it happened, these two districts were worked by a large number of "senior men." Because they had suffered fewer layoffs in the cut that day and because the senior men had more to lose by striking, these two districts were less likely to support such a protest.

Nespoli got in his VW and headed uptown to talk to them.

The senior men could get shafted if they supported us, but they felt it wasn't right how the city was treating us. I knew a lot of senior guys in the garages from the football team, so that helped out in talking to them.

John O'Keefe, a Shop Steward in Manhattan who was instrumental in reaching across two boroughs and, more importantly, bridge an important generational divide. "Guys on the job, senior men – I had all the telephone numbers – and they all came out," remembers O'Keefe. Getting the senior men to back the action was an essential ingredient for success. It was the same generational gap that had been bridged seven years earlier, sparking the Strike of 1968. The Union headquarters wanted no part of this protest. As Nespoli pointed out

The [union] business agents were against it. So they stayed in the union hall... they did not want to get beat up. And DeLury had started to fade by then. DeLury was, well, he was a one-man band.

John DeLury did not call for or control this action, but still it was intimated in the press and Department that he was calling the shots. In fact, with his health deteriorating, DeLury played a far lesser role than in the 1968 strike and limited himself to putting the best face on the situation, for himself and the Union. Still, Sanitation Commissioner Robert T. Groh sarcastically described the 3-day job action as "the best-organized wildcat strike I have ever seen." The wildcat ended when the USA negotiated an unusual agreement by offering to loan $1.6 million in Union funds so that the laid-off workers could be temporarily rehired. It was a last-ditch efort by the Union in the hope that an alternative to the layoffs would be found. Despite the fact that the Union had not supported the action, it was Local 831's duty to help find a solution and to do everything possible to retain the jobs of the laid-off Sanmen.

A wildcat strike is usually defined as taking place without the approval of union officials. Wildcatters, however, seize control not of the union, but of a situation. In fact, a wildcat can be seen as an act of pure unionism and one

A defiant Sanman, dressed in civilian clothes, stands beside his truck during the 1975 wildcat. The term "Stink City" is written on the sign and is a throwback to the 1968 strike, a description that arose in contrast to Mayor Lindsay's public relations efforts to call it "Fun City."

125

that injects the union with new vitality. A wildcat allows the rank and file to state most strongly: "We are the Union."

That is true even more in the case of the Uniformed Sanitationmen's Association, where all the members are Sanmen and where all the officials come from the ranks of Sanmen. In Local 831, union power flows from the bottom up as much as from the top down. Where union officials look for long-term improvements through collective bargaining, wildcatters seek immediate results through collective action. It was the rank and file, and not John DeLury, who called for the strikes of 1968 and 1960. Although seldom referred to as such, both of those strikes were wildcats. When the system fails – whether the blame is on labor or management – and the rank and file exercises its right of refusing to work, every action becomes a wildcat.

Down for the Count

In New York City of 1975, all kinds of systems – not the least of which involved labor relations – were failing. The actual event was called a "Fiscal Crisis," but it was more a crisis of confidence. The City had for the previous twenty years exercised some very creative accounting in order to camouflage increased operating costs in a time of decreasing revenues. Money coming into the city coffers was down as a result of the "white flight" to suburbia and a loss of manufacturing jobs. Money going out was up through the roof as the demand for city services, especially social services and welfare, had grown with an influx of immigrants and a surge in the population of urban poor and also the aging. The resulting shortfall ran into the billions. Banks refused to rollover city loans. In a knee-jerk reaction, City Hall cut the payroll of municipal employees and reduced city services.

Of course, a cutback in services provided did not mean a reduction in the demand for those services. The result became frustrated citizens. Besides having their compensation take a hit, Sanmen were now blamed for dirtier streets from the loss of manpower. Residential areas that usually were assigned three pickups per week were now allocated just one; some congested areas that formerly received six pickups a week now had three. Some homeowners and residents of the city openly cursed at Sanmen, demanding better service. A much-reduced force struggled to clean up the added load of 58,000 tons of refuse left over from the action. Sanmen were getting no respect from city bosses or residents. Even Commissioner Groh became a whipping boy for Mayor Beame who told him to "clean up the streets or else." By October, Groh cited "pressure" as the reason for his leaving and the parade of thirteen Sanitation Commissioners over a ten- year period continued.

Wildcats were not limited to Sanitationmen. Municipal unions which had in the prior decade only just started to satisfy the nearly hundred-year old demands of their rank-and-file were now made the scapegoats for the city's mounting debt. The pressure had been building for years, so when Mayor

■ Wildcat!

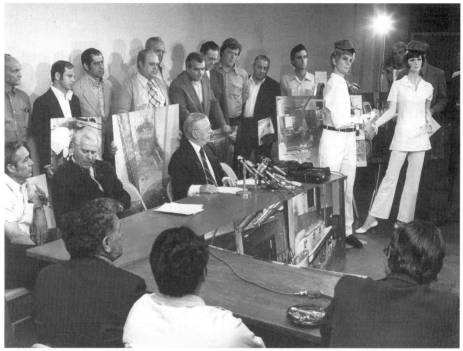

Bigel and DeLury outdo each other in their mocking of City plans to bring in "the privates," here represented by two fashionably dressed manikins.

Beame laid off 19,000 city employees in June 1975, the lid was ready to blow off the City's kettle of labor relations. Beame said that another 21,000 layoffs could be expected in the next month. More wildcat actions broke out across the city.

On the same day of the Sanmen's wildcat, July 1, an angry crowd of 500 laid-off policemen, dressed in civilian clothes, set up barricades and blocked traffic on the Brooklyn Bridge. These "ex-policemen" proceeded to let the air out of car tires, and argue with the stopped motorists. According to the Times, they "hurled beer cans and bottles and shouted obscenities at uniformed officers and commanders who pleaded with them to clear the roadways." One newly dismissed officer said: "I'm desperate. It's our survival and we've been double-crossed."

On July 2, a similar situation occurred when 570 newly laid-off highway workers picketed and stopped traffic on the Henry Hudson Parkway. Even more tie-ups and snarls occurred at drawbridges in Brooklyn and Queens where layoffs of workers disrupted operations.

Unfortunately, two weeks later, the announcement came that 1,434 Sanmen were being laid off. Those still working were stretched to the limit as the Department struggled to reorganize its force. Some 183 Sanitation

Smoke pours from a car during Wildcat action of 1975.

officers were demoted to work on the streets. Morale hit a low as remaining actives were sent to work in unfamiliar neighborhoods, under the supervision of new "bosses."

For Local 831, there was much at stake. Many of the gains that John DeLury and the USA had made since the action of 1968 were in danger, but contract negotiations came around almost every year and the Union was confident of its ability to collectively bargain. What the Union really feared losing was the respect that had taken decades to achieve and that was now in jeopardy as the situation rapidly deteriorated in 1975.

20-year Pension in Trouble

The USA had bigger worries than the police. By 1973, the State Pension Commission was recommending cuts in pensions to public employees that would turn the clock back twenty years. Sixteen public employee unions, representing 600,000 members, formed a coalition to fight the "anti-pension scheme."

In a nod to his status as a respected labor leader and trailblazer for public pensions, John DeLury was appointed spokesman for the group, called the New York State Conference of Public Employee Organizations. DeLury immediately announced that the unions would "enter the political arena" in order to protect their members. At the same time, Jack Bigel was appointed chief consultant to the group. Theirs was a team that had consistently achieved results.

Bigel described the new pension plan as "without question, one of the most complicated plans in the entire public sector." If the new pension program went through, it would create what he called a "double standard of wages with two different wages for people working side-by-side and reduce retirement benefits by about 40-50%."

The State Pension Commission was also recommending cuts in retirement benefits because of Social Security, and additional reductions in death benefits as well as disability benefits. The unions had a fight on their hands. Unfortunately, it came right at a time when New York City's fiscal problems took center stage.

The City's financial mess was made worse by a national recession that hit the United States in 1973. Inflation was out of control and President Nixon installed wage and price controls. By 1974, New York City's debt had grown to more than $10 billion, and one-third of it consisted of short-term notes that needed to be rolled over each year by the lending banks. Mayor Abe Beame waffled on budget cuts and promised layoffs of City employees in the fall of 1974. As a result, he lost the confidence of the banks and financial institutions.

By early 1975, the Mayor had also lost the confidence of the public unions. DC 37's Victor Gotbaum and Local 237's Barry Feinstein warned the city not to "balance the budget on the backs of the workers." They accused the banks of precipitating the fiscal crisis by demanding high interest rates. Ten thousand union members marched on Wall Street on June 4, 1975 and massed in front of the First National City Bank, singling it out and denouncing it. Gotbaum and Feinstein threatened to withdraw $175 million in pension funds from the bank's cash account.

Such a move might have rattled the First National, but would have done little good for a city in need. Jack Bigel, the foremost expert on pensions, also thought in terms of withdrawal, but, with his usual strategic thinking, had in mind a clear idea of what to do with the money. Save the City or, as the pragmatic Bigel might have put it, lend the city enough money in order to get it out of hock to the banks.

Meanwhile, the City, the State, the Federal Government and all the banks – four players in total – could not figure out how to put the city's financial humpty-dumpty back together again. City employees deferred $200 million in wages for three years, but that was little more than handing a bandaid to a City hemorrhaging money. There would be no cavalry arriving from the nation's capitol, either. In October 1975, President Gerald Ford, in response to the Mayor's request for a federal guaranty, gave cause for one of the most memorable front headlines ever: "Ford to City – Drop Dead."

Within a month, Bigel had convinced the city's union leaders that their best option was to use Union pensions to purchase $2.5 billion in city bonds. This was much more than a stop-gap measure and produced the one thing that New York was in need of more than money itself: confidence in the City.

NEW YORK DAILY NEWS

A police officer watching as uncollected trash burns during the Wildcat action of 1975.

A financial plan was devised and the federal government eventually coughed up a loan. The banks bought back into the City, but only after Jack Bigel helped smoothed things over between them and the city's unions. Jimmy Carter's inauguration as president in 1977 also nurtured the hope that more help would be forthcoming from Washington. It did, but slowly. Although the Fiscal Crisis would start to ease up by 1978, the catastrophic effects on the city's budget and the bite that it took out of civil service employees would linger through the mid-1980s.

Bigel later described the situation as "playing craps with the Unions' pensions." Though to the extent that the city unions were part of the city, they were betting on themselves, and that would have seemed a fairly smart bet. Besides, the alternative, as all the unions knew, was to stand idly by and watch the city go down the toilet, at which point they would certainly have regretted not taking a higher stake in the outcome.

During this time, the city's unions, both uniformed and non-uniformed, came together in the form of the Municipal Labor Committee. They put feuding aside to solve a common problem. Relations eased between the unions.

For its part, the USA fought to regain the jobs of all the Sanmen who had been laid off in 1975. By 1977, almost half were back on the job. The overall picture, however, was still bleak as job attrition and tight budgets would become the rule for the next ten years. The Union had won the 20-year pension in 1967 only to have it taken away in 1973 and now was given little hope for its return any time soon.

Local 831's emphasis on productivity remained the one bright spot. Although the Fiscal Crisis stalled Delury and Bigel's goal of implementing productivity into Sanitationmen's contracts, there was a breakthrough in April 1977, when Local 831 finally succeeded in obtaining a productivity provision retroactive to July 1976. The two-year contract provided that "the Sanitationmen and the City would share in any savings from productivity programs that are in excess of the savings necessary to pay for cost-of-living adjustments. This "innovative gain-sharing clause," as it was referred to by the Times, "precipitated immediate protests from leaders of other municipal unions, who rushed to City Hall to demand similar treatment."

First Deputy Mayor Donald Kummersfeld emphasized that "the City really hasn't given away anything" and could only gain from the arrangement. As the Union reported in its own USA Record, "labor consultant Jack Bigel was the architect of the gainsharing proposal... and he had been pushing hard for the 50-50 split."

This was the first concrete step toward what came to be called the USA's "productivity program." By the time Ed Koch took office as Mayor in January 1978, the concept of incentives based on gainsharing for the City Sanitationmen was a given. While other city unions had a long slog ahead some dark stretches of the Fiscal Crisis, the Uniformed Sanitationmen's Association was already holding up productivity as if it were a candle in the darkness.

There was another candle, however, that Sanmen would be holding up soon, by the light of which they would look into their past and remember the man who had helped them come so far. John Delury, after retiring in 1978 after four decades at the helm, died on February 12, 1980. The man who, together with five fellow dump laborers, had forged from the fires of a City incinerator one of the great municipal unions in New York City, had finally passed from the scene.

His legacy was to ensure that the Union would not, especially in those troubled times, give back what had taken so long to achieve.

Chapter Ten

The Two Man Truck – Take It or Leave It?

"Can you really discuss productivity with a workforce that is being harassed, that is being hounded, that is being threatened...? Is that the way you get productivity, by massive, lethal injections of insecurity?"

- USA consultant Jack Bigel, speaking before the Impasse Hearing on the Two-Man Truck, Nov. 28, 1980

By the Numbers

As with productivity, so much of the life of a Sanitation Worker is about numbers. Number of stops, number of tons, number of workers to perform the job, number of minutes for breaks and lunch, number of dollars gained by meeting productivity goals: all these are constantly added, subtracted and multiplied by the worker matching personal performance to the job, by the human being weighing reality against expectations.

It is no surprise that Jack Bigel, a numbers guru himself, should have called Sanitationmen "very practical mathematicians." Or, as the legendary labor attorney Charles Moerdler said, "I'll take a Sanitationman over a fiscal expert any day."

As to the number of men that had worked a truck for as long as anyone could remember, it was three: one driver, two loaders. If, as some believe, there is magic in numbers, that could explain how a team of only three Sanmen was able to perform the trick of making 18,000-plus pounds of garbage disappear from the streets of New York City on a daily basis.

On the practical side, teams of three gave Sanmen certain options. If not magic, then there was at least safety in numbers. Three men allowed for

Jimmy Alongi (2nd from Left) and Harry Nespoli (3rd from Left) at a San garage, explain the coming reality of the two man truck.

greater rotation of who was driving and who was loading. When one man was under the weather or, as it happened, forced by the Department to return to work before he had fully recovered from injuries suffered on the job, the other two men could put their backs into it a little more and cover for their hurting partner. Also, three men were able to look out for each other and maintain a closer watch on their truck and equipment, which was often in disrepair and required constant fiddling. They could also keep a better eye on the surrounding city, always full of surprises. And not just for their own sake: many a Sanman has stopped a fire; chased down a criminal; and rescued a citizen in distress.

In the end, a team of three meant decisions were more like group decisions; it meant a degree of power in their mobile workplace; it meant control over their jobs and, even more, over their own lives.

By the start of 1980, City Hall wanted to change all that. In the name of cost-cutting, in the name of the ongoing Fiscal Crisis, in the name of what they called productivity, the Department of Sanitation announced they had ordered 250 two-man side-loading trucks. The Department insisted these trucks were safer than the old rear-loading trucks and would require only two men to do a job previously performed by three. The Union did not trust the Department, which tried to support its case for the truck based on little more than the manufacturer's brochure. One man would have to go. Outright firing of personnel would not be necessary. Instead, the cuts would likely be made via that slow death known as attrition. The only thing that stood in the way was Local 831.

With each passing week in 1980, a rumbling grew louder on the streets of Gotham. To City Hall's ear, it was the thunder of the two-man trucks rolling toward the city. From where the Union stood, however, the rumbling could be traced to a different source, straight back to 7,200 angry Sanmen, fed up with nothing but wage cuts and other setbacks since the Fiscal Crisis of 1975, and who now saw the two-man truck as the next serious threat to their jobs.

Sparks flew on both sides. Union versus City Hall. Man against Machine.

Putting the Brakes on the Two-Man Truck

Local 831 was neither slow nor shy in expressing its disapproval of the use of a two-man truck to the bosses. President Eddie Ostrowski, who had taken over for DeLury, voiced the USA's position: "No way! The city is asking for trouble. If they try to put the two-man truck into operation, they're just going to be lined up and stay there. We've ordered our members not to man them."

Although the Union took a hard line on the two-man truck, Ostrowski and Jack Bigel could see the writing on the wall. Bigel knew first-hand that the city, although no longer on the brink of bankruptcy, was still a long way from full financial recovery. City Hall's threats to privatize residential collection might not be taken at face value, but the two-man truck was a different animal. Bigel convinced Ostrowski that the most the union could do was slow down the introduction of the truck and, in the meantime, negotiate the best possible conditions and wage increases for the Sanmen who would be affected by it.

Reality set in at the end of January 1980 when city officials put out a Request for Bid on the two-man trucks. Ostrowski maintained the trucks were unsafe and needed to be negotiated with the Union. Commissioner Norman Steisel, of course, argued the opposite, that the trucks were safe and that no such negotiations needed to take place. The final showdown took place in Jack Bigel's office. In a meeting with Bigel, Deputy Mayor Nat Leventhal announced that the trucks had been ordered and the Union could do nothing about it. According to Bigel's associate, Allen Brawer, the feisty Bigel walked to the window and, looking out beyond the city, puffed on his pipe and tossed a challenge over his shoulder to the Deputy Mayor: "You're going to bring the trucks in? Good! I encourage you to. But I can't say they're going to survive once they reach the streets of New York." Without waiting for an answer, they moved on. The issue was over.

The Two-Man Truck – No Turning Back

By the time the 'first batch' of two-man trucks entered the city limits, Local 831 and City Hall had each other in a headlock. Despite one hundred meetings over the previous 11 months, both sides failed to reach an agreement. This impasse meant that, in December 1980, the USA and the Department of Sanitation were forced to submit to arbitration. The purpose of this was for a neutral arbitrator to hear arguments from the DOS as to why it felt justified in bringing in the two-man truck; and for the USA to explain its refusal to allow its members to use that truck before the terms for its use had been negotiated.

On each team, the Union's and the Department's, were seven men, all highly competent, all seasoned veterans. It looked to be an evenly matched event, except for one noteworthy factor: the USA had Jack Bigel, a man who had wrestled in college and, in many ways, ever since. The hearing lasted an entire day and, although both sides presented solid arguments, there was never any doubt who commanded the mat at City Hall on November 28, 1980.

Before the pleasantries of a meeting were even out of the way, Bigel was on offense. His strategy at times involved the actual use of the introduction as the first attempt to attack and throw the opponent off-balance. Bigel's associates Tony Gajda and Allen Brawer took turns on offense for Local 831 throughout the rest of the hearing. Scarlatos and Ostrowski played key roles, especially in emphasizing the unknowns and potential dangers of the new truck. Tony Gajda summarized the USA's concern by pointing out the already high rate of injury among Sanmen.

The foundation of the Union's presentation rested on the following: whatever the City saved as a result of the introduction of the two-man truck should be shared with the workers who help realize those savings. This was based on the indisputable facts that the new truck would both increase the workload and possibly present new dangers to Sanmen. The Union argued that sharing the gains in therefore, should be viewed as fair and just compensation, and not as a one-time bonus.

Arbitrator's Report – the City Gains, the City Shares

The arbitrator agreed with the Union. Professor Matthew Kelly recommended a $11 a shift differential for Sanmen working the new two-man side-loading trucks. This would amount to an approximate $2,000 annual

Eddie Ostrowski at a press conference on the Uniformed Forces Coalition – representing Sanitationmen, police, fire, and corrections. Bigel puffs on his pipe, strategizing.

increase for those workers. It was less than the Union and Bigel had asked for and, at the same time, more than they realistically expected, given the still-healing financial condition of the city. In addition, the panel ruled that the City could use two men on the old three-men trucks, so long as those men were also paid the $11 differential.

Kelly, in his ruling, noted the increased workload and recognized the "tough and hazardous" work of Sanitationmen. He also noted that other cities, in reducing the crew size due to the implementation of two-man trucks, were also providing a salary differential to the affected workers.

Director of Labor Relations Bruce McIver was bothered by the size of the differential. Sanitation Commissioner Norman Steisel, however, was enthusiastic about the finding and focused on the possible productivity savings which he called "substantial."

Allen Brawer comments on the obstacles the Union encountered in setting up the program:

At first, everyone was suspicious... the Sanmen, the City. The

137

two-man truck was a concession. What we [the Union] got in return… was much more important – agreement by the City on gainsharing. When you think about it, this was a revolutionary concept – the City sharing the dollar savings from greater productivity with the workers. This was Jack Bigel's brilliance, his ability to play ball with the devil if it got the Union five cents an hour.

The standoff over the two-man truck became a constant background noise – sometimes very loud – for other ongoing threats to Local 831. City Hall continued to beat the war drums with its two-fisted threats to privatize and civilianize job functions, not to mention a shockingly low offer on a wage increase. All these things got piled onto the bonfire of municipal labor relations as the USA, its first quarter century behind it, headed into the 1980s.

To Walk Like a Man

At the same time, however, the Union needed to take care of its everyday business, usually showing up in the form of a thousand small fires called grievances. Although many long-term concerns such as improvements to pension and health plans required persistent efforts, it was the issue of grievances that occupied most of the Union's time and attention on a day-to-day basis.

No matter how minor a grievance may have seemed, it assumed major importance to the Union for two primary reasons. First of all, aggrieved rank and file members simply expected that the Union step up to their defense. Second, the Department itself expected it. This adversarial structure was, after all, one of the primary ways that the union and the Department defined their relationship to each other. In that sense, each time it stood up for the rank and file, the Union was also fighting for its own degree of respect from the Department.

Their Union's readiness to go to the mat for them over grievances meant as much to Sanmen as wage increases and fringe benefits. No other issue did more to determine their daily quality of life.

The 1980s – A Decade of Greed

The 1980s would eventually come to be known as "The Greed Decade." It did not start off that way. In January 1980 the country was in a recession, inflation was barreling along like a runaway freight train, and interest rates were sky-high. Union membership was also suffering and in slow decline throughout the United States.

Municipal unions, including the Uniformed Sanitationmen's Association, were drawing a line in the sand between themselves and City Hall. Over the previous five years, City employees had endured losses to inflation and watched fringe benefits slip away. The spiraling cost of living meant that a Sanman's paycheck in 1980 bought 15% less than it had just three years earlier. With contracts coming up for renewal in June, many of the city's unions were dusting off their armor and getting ready, once again, to fight for pay increases, something that the Fiscal Crisis had turned into a dirty word.

Sanmen Lead the Way for Uniformed Forces

The three unions representing police, fire and Sanitationmen, calling themselves the Uniformed Forces Coalition, had Mayor Koch and his aides worried. The heads of the three unions made clear that the City's offer – 4% – would mean a real cut, given the high inflation and cost of living increases of the time. To accept it would have meant more backsliding for the city's uniformed forces.

The coalition, which had become a foursome with the addition of the correction officers union, set a deadline of July 1 for the City to present to them acceptable terms. If the City missed that deadline, they threatened a strike. Speaking for the Coalition, Ostrowski stated:

The City has asked us to make sacrifices during the last five years. Now it is time for the City to open its purse strings and give us what we are due. Through this coalition, the first in the city's history of the uniformed services, we will present a strong and united front. We have seen our paychecks shrink because of inflation and we won't let this happen anymore. We'll do whatever is necessary to get what we deserve."

That was his official coalition stance, cool in tone. Ostrowski could get more passionate when he spoke on behalf of Sanmen who took the offer of 4% as a personal insult. Ostrowski described them as "ready to go off like a stick of dynamite."

The coalition increased the clout of the uniformed forces at a time that they could feel the walls of the City's budget closing in around them. Their solidarity and threat of a general strike was the most effective weapon at their disposal at that time. Such a strike action by these essential service unions – all at the same time – would virtually shut the city down. Ostrowski spoke for the entire Coalition when he said: "I don't want to go out on strike and I'm sure the public is not going to like to see this coalition go on strike. If there is a strike, the Mayor creates a strike, whichever Mayor is sitting there."

Of the four uniformed unions, the USA had the most to gain from the increased visibility that the coalition provided. The police, fire and corrections

U.S.A. Vice-president Jimmy Condon (seated second from left) leads a spirited discussion. After DeLury's retirement, Condon was defeated in the union election and Peter Scarlatos became the new Vice-president.

unions were concerned primarily with getting long overdue increases in contract renewals. Eddie Ostrowski and the city's Sanmen had that – and a lot more – to worry about.

A Triple Threat

Fighting to jack up the City's offer from 4% to "double numbers," as Ostrowski put it, was enough to keep any union working overtime. The USA, however, was doing something more like double shifts, since they had to fend off – at the same time – the attack of the two-man truck, a new threat to privatize, and the same old enemy of civilianization.

In May 1980 City Comptroller Harrison J. Goldin suggested that the City eliminate uniformed Sanitationmen from all jobs other than cleaning streets and collecting garbage. The Comptroller made no mention of snow removal, but it was typical of City officials, in late spring when snow is no longer a threat, to forget that this is one of the crucially important functions of New

York City Sanitationmen.

What the City did not speak of was the long-standing arrangement that certain of these "civilian" jobs, which the Union referred to as "tissue" jobs, were reserved for and performed by Sanitationmen who had become injured in the field and were no longer physically capable of handling a route.

Eddie Ostrowski shot back at the comptroller's civilianization effort in stating that "the timing of the report just two months before our contract is up is very suspect."

Given the Coalition's announced deadline of July 1, it was looking more and more like fireworks that July would be starting a few days before the Fourth.

The Uniformed Forces Coalition Prepares to Strike

As the deadline of July 1 drew near, the Uniformed Forces Coalition were about to make good on their promise of a strike if the City would not budge. In an eleventh-hour effort to work out a deal, the Coalition gave the City a couple of additional days to consider, or face the possibility of a strike on July 3. The City interpreted this as a sign that the Coalition was bluffing.

The Coalition responded by holding a mass rally at Louis Armstrong Stadium in Queens on Tuesday, July 1. Over 7,000 rank and file uniformed force members – police, fire, Sanitationmen and corrections – showed up and kicked things off by singing "10 and more or out the door!" The song referred to their demand for a pay increase of at least 10%. The crowd roared approval of the new deadline as well as of the show of solidarity exhibited by the different unions and labor leaders that day.

One Sanman carried a placard that read in bold letters:

> **Extra! Extra! Extra!**
> **Cop Shot! Fireman Killed!**
> **Sanitationman Injured!**
> **We Risk Our Lives –**
> **We Deserve More!**

City Hall announced its intention to bring in 600 State Troopers in the event of a strike. There was once again the call for the National Guard – just as had taken place during the sanitation strike of 1968. As the situation teetered on the brink, it became clear that the City had absolutely no plan – contingency or otherwise – for handling a strike by all 42,000 members of the police, fire, sanitation, and corrections department.

Final maneuvering by both sides led to the City caving and agreeing to a wage increase of 9% the first year, and 8% the second year. The uniformed forces declared victory for themselves. The 17% increase would at least allow

Sanmen to catch up with inflation and cost of living increases over the last two years. The real difference consisted of improvements in city contributions to welfare funds, cost-of-living allowances and also uniform allowances, which was of great importance to uniformed forces who were often forced to dig deep into their own pockets in order to outfit themselves properly.

All together, with these additional "extras" and benefits, Local 831 was able to translate it as an overall 21% pay increase. Ostrowski commented: "We have lived up to our pledge to our members. We put the bread on the table...and have brought back a good contract considering the fiscal plight of the city."

The contract allowed the Union a little breathing room, enabling it to shift gears and to address the other three fronts of privatization, civilianization and the two-man truck.

No to "Privates!"

Meanwhile, the City tried to put teeth in its threat to privatize by commissioning a study of eight other cities across the United States to show they paid much less for municipal sanitation than did New York City. Jack Bigel called the City's study "rigged." Bigel shot down the City's study by producing his own analysis that pointed out the unfair and uneven nature of the comparison, given the special demands of sanitation in New York City. He pointed out the number and variety of jobs that were assigned to NYC Sanmen. Bigel's report put special emphasis on Sanmen's job of snow removal, something that their "counterparts" in other cities did not undertake.

The Union mounted a campaign to remind the public of the negative aspects of privatization, among them the Mob and an even greater risk of strikes by private unions. Ostrowski together with Vice-President Peter Scarlatos, Recording Secretary Robert Kelly, Treasurer Val Pappa and Trustees Harry Nespoli, John O'Keefe and Jimmy Alongi, all became familiar faces at Community Board hearings and paid visits to all the borough Presidents throughout the summer and into the fall of 1980.

Survival or Civilians?

As for civilianization, Ostrowski got it in a headlock and would not let go. As a Sanitationman who himself had been severely injured and required "tissue duty" during his recovery, the USA President knew first-hand the importance of stopping the City from giving these clerical jobs away. The USA released figures showing that in 1978-1979, one out of every two Sanmen suffered an injury on the job, a total of 3,651 injuries for 7,200 sanitation workers. Even Commissioner Steisel, known for his considerable brainpower, could not dispute the USA's numbers and publicly disagreed with City Hall's attempt at a civilian blitz.

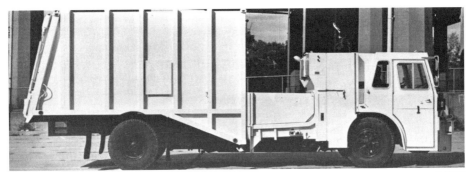

Photo of original two man truck... it was as inefficient as it was ugly.

Bonus – Privates Off the Table for Two Years

The Union achieved an added bonus that took many people by surprise – an agreement by the Koch administration to postpone for two years any plans to privatize. The City announced that they were delaying it in order to "create a favorable labor relations climate" in order to sweeten the deal for the Union to accept the two-man truck.

Most importantly, the Union sought and received in the arbitration award agreement by the City to set up of a Three-Person Dispute Resolution Panel to handle labor-management disputes. Jack Bigel, in arguing for the new panel, relied on a clause that had been inserted in every sanitation contract since the strike of 1968 that states the need to set up a labor-management committee. This clause came in handy in 1980.

In "selling" the two-man truck to the men on the street, Ostrowski, Scarlatos, and Nespoli referred more and more to the Productivity Program as a whole. Productivity had been part of their vocabulary for a long time already, but now, as the Union moved toward its next quarter-century, the value of turning it into a program was clear to see.

Productivity remained a very hot topic for management in the 1980s. Allen Brawer describes that time and Local 831's approach to productivity: "Here in New York City was a Union pushing the standards. In the rest of America, management was using productivity and pushing the standards. It was almost crazy, but it wasn't – it was brilliant."

Besides, the nature of Sanmen's jobs required them to stay one step ahead of the City. It seemed only fitting that the Productivity Program would help them remain there. The Union had succeeded in moving forward against tough odds, just as they had been for more than a century. Now they stayed on their toes, never forgetting one other principle in wrestling: the best time to move again is right after a successful move. Or, as Jack Bigel liked to say: "Looking back only gives you a stiff neck."

Acceptance of the two-man truck by the Union – and the differential payment made by the City – meant that, for the first time in history, the City would give back to workers a direct share of the savings created by those workers' increased productivity. It rang in a coming revolution not just for Sanitationmen, but for all New York City civil servants.

Chapter Eleven

Stepping Up to the Plate

"Shouldn't you cut an analyst before you cut a Sanitationman?"
- Sanitation Commissioner Norman Steisel, on the announced cuts in the number of Sanmen October 24, 1982

ollowing in the footsteps of John DeLury was like going to bat after Babe Ruth. But Edward "Eddie O" Ostrowski, who had played AAA ball for Elmira after WWII before he became a Sanman in 1953, knew his way around the Union bases. In twenty-five years he went from Shop Steward to Recording Secretary to Treasurer to his finally becoming President of Local 831 in 1978. Peter Scarlatos, who had run on the Condon ticket for the office of Vice-President and won, along with newly elected Trustee Harry Nespoli, brought new blood to the Union leadership.

Athletes All

A tradition of athleticism had prevailed in the Uniformed Sanitationmen's Association from the beginning. John DeLury at age 63 could still jump like a gymnast to the top of a sound truck during the 1968 Strike. Al Katz, a union consultant, was a Golden Gloves quarter-finalist, Jack Bigel was a wrestler and who kept going to the mat until the day he died, and Harry Nespoli, who was a new trustee in 1980, was good enough on the football field to be signed by the New York Jets farm team. And the average Sanman was, by the very nature of the job, a professional weightlifter.

They were a scrappy bunch and well-suited to the times, since it was little more than scraps that the City was putting on the table as it continued its long slow crawl out of the fiscal mess of the 1970s. The Union's motto had always been "Never give anything back," but the rank and file, like all New York City's civil servants, had lost considerable ground in the area of wages

Constant alertness is required in order to negotiate a street sweeper around many obstacles. Here a car is parked where it should not be.

alone between 1975-1980 and had its hands full trying to stop the backsliding going into the new decade. Every time the Union brought up salary increases, the City cried poormouth and pointed to the Financial Control Board that continued to look over its shoulder until 1986. Every Union victory – whether on the front of wages or benefits or working conditions – came at a high cost. It seemed that for every two steps forward during these times, Local 831 was forced to take at least one step backward.

By 1980, Edward Ostrowski had found his game, arguing for an increase in the number of Sanitationmen, dealing with grievances, sitting down with the City on constant contract go-arounds, trying to win pension improvements, and trying to even the playing field with the Department.

In the early 1980s, one piece of business dominated the union's everyday agenda: "selling" the two-man truck. The Union had agreed to try out the truck; they did not yet agree to it wholesale. It remained to be seen if the truck worked as advertised and, more importantly, if it was safe. The only way to find out was to put the two-man truck on the streets and have some of the men work it.

Many rank and file were deadset against the two-man truck. Like salesman traveling door-to-door, Pete Scarlatos and Harry Nespoli – Ostrowski's two lieutenants – had to take the campaign to the streets, roll call after roll call, garage by garage. Before work, during breaks and lunch, and after work, Scarlatos and Nespoli mounted a full-tilt campaign to educate Sanmen on the potential benefits of the new truck. Some were more open-minded; others refused the notion of breaking up their three-man teams.

Since only a limited number of districts would get a share of the first small batch of 160 trucks, Nespoli and Scarlatos could cut some slack to those garages that absolutely refused, and hope that they would see the light later on. Nespoli recalled those bargaining sessions later: "Once I even found myself flipping a coin with one garage. Heads – you don't take the truck for six months, tails – you take it now. It came up heads. Most of the time, though, you could talk reason with the guys... and the shift differential, the extra money, helped. Before that I thought I knew what negotiating was... It was only then that I learned what real negotiating was."

There was resistance to the new truck – or the shift differential anyway – from outside the Union as well. Police and fire took notice of the $11 differential – which could add up to $2,000 to a Sanman's yearly salary – and did not like what they saw. The shift differential was going to "break the relationship" that had kept Sanmen forever earning less than their uniformed brothers. The new Productivity Program was going to allow a Sanman's salary to approach or even exceed that of police and fire for the first time ever. The PBA and UFA voiced their displeasure, but could do little in the face of the overwhelming support for productivity increases from many different quarters.

Not only did the City bask in the "productivity revolution," but the press spoke universally in favor of it as well. The New York Times editorialized: "The honeymoon spirit of the Sanitation Workers' agreement is based on gains by both sides." Many voices suggested that similar productivity programs should be introduced into other segments of the civil service, including police and fire.

Problems With The New Truck Design

Meanwhile, the new two-man truck had design problems: structural weaknesses in its frame. The trucks were immediately recalled for rewelding and the installation of reinforcing metal plates. Then other problems popped up. The trucks were supposed to carry up to 12.5 tons. Because of hydraulic problems, it turned out they could only carry 7.5 tons. This would mean a major added expense from extra trips to landfills and transfer stations in order to get dump their load.

Many Sanmen complained that the two-man truck was more aggravation than it was worth and the only way productivity was happening was on their backs – literally. With the force cut back, the city was getting dirtier and, as always, accusing fingers pointed at Sanmen . The City's measure of cleanliness went from a rating of 76.8% one year earlier to 73.7% in April 1981. The Department employed ten full-time inspectors who rated the city from 1 ("Absolutely spotless, not a tissue") to 7 ("filthiest possible"). In the pre-Fiscal Crisis of the early 1970s, 2,500 Sanitationmen had been dedicated exclusively to street cleaning (as opposed to garbage collection). By 1981, less than a third that number – 800 men in total – were required to do the same job. Try as they might, the result could never be the same. No matter how efficient garbage collection, it was by the cleanliness of the streets that Sanmen were judged.

The Rat Squad

Turning up the heat, the Department put a new control mechanism on the men. A new policy required Sanmen who were sick or injured to stay home. Departmental agents, or the "Rat Squad" as they were called by the Union, started making surprise visits them to make sure they were home. If a Sanman was out picking up his child from school or buying a bottle of milk at the store, and the Rat Squad came while he was out, then the Sanman lost his sick pay and faced more disciplinary action. The Big Brother treatment wasn't limited to the sick and injured. "Internal inspections" of men at work increased as well. Kevin Blanch, a Sanitationman from Staten Island, said, "They'll watch one truck all day. The second you take a five-minute break – Bang! – they jump on you."

In an article in the New York Times, journalist Colin Campbell described the morale problem, detailing in particular the "grim" working conditions of Sanmen.

> By all accounts, the garages, which are the Sanitationmen's frequent work places, range from rundown to primitive.

> Ruinous work places... are a constant sore on the Sanitationman's self-image, and current rehabilitation efforts strike many as negligible.

> A recent visit to the large day-and-night garage at 12th Avenue at 56th Street showed that a single bare light bulb over an expanse of lockers had recently been augmented with other bulbs.

> But the locker room was still grim. The lockers were rusty castoffs from other city departments. Several toilets in the nearby men's room did not flush. Most of the toilet stalls lacked doors. There was no toilet paper at all. The only drinking water came from some broken faucets on an ancient sink. The showers were filthy.

> Plumbing concerns the men not just because they sometimes

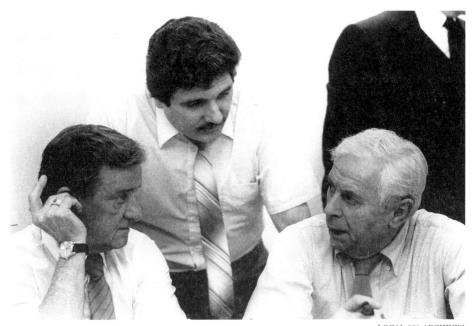

A familiar trio inside – and outside – the Union Hall. Left to Right, Local 831 President Edward Ostrowski, Vice-President Peter Scarlatos and consultant Jack Bigel.

cannot find toilets while on the job – restaurants have been known to ask Sanitationmen to leave – but also because they would rather not go home reeking.

The men groaned. The new truck was a lemon, working conditions still stunk and the Union was still fighting an uphill battle to get wages where they were five years earlier, before the Fiscal Crisis. But the Uniformed Sanitationmen's Association had never been good at sitting still. Instead, its leadership exercised a long tradition of organizational education and political involvement that was almost unmatched in New York.

In that spirit, the USA put together the first-ever Shop Stewards Conference in upstate New York in September 1981. Nearly three-hundred shop stewards attended the weekend-long event that featured sessions on collective bargaining, pension reform, current political action, and updates on the two-man truck and still new Productivity Program. Guests included USA Attorney Charles Moerdler, labor leaders Victor Gotbaum of DC 37 and Barry Feinstein, President of Teamsters Local 237 and, from the city side, Commissioner Steisel and Mayor Koch. It was a relaxed atmosphere for all parties, management as well as labor, to put their heads together and ask what was working and what was not. Cameras caught Jack Bigel looking almost relaxed.

Barry Feinstein stressed the importance of getting rid of the Tier-3 retirement system, which would force Sanmen to work twice as long – up to age 62 – before it could be collected. Feinstein pledged his union's solidarity with the USA in their mutual fight to get the 20-year pension back. Norman Steisel assured the union that the next batch of two-man trucks would have substantial revisions made to them. Ed Koch promised his support for the long-term rehabilitation of the Department's garages. Charles Moerdler, taking advantage of Steisel and Koch's presence, let loose with both guns at the Department's antique and biased system of justice that still prevailed over disciplinary matters and that ruled over the work lives of Sanmen.

I'm disgusted with the abuse of the legal procedures in the trial room. I've never been so disgusted. The worst criminal would get a better shake. The Department is the judge, jury and executioner. Why not give these men a fair shake?

The Shop Stewards also got the chance that weekend to meet Robert Schrank, one of the gurus of modern labor-management theory and, more to the point, the first Chairman of the Tripartite Panel, the mechanism that ruled over the entire Productivity Program. Schrank discussed the impact of the new Reagan economy and its effect on both Sanitationmen and the labor movement in general. Schrank told the stewards that "the labor movement has to think in a new way, because management is saying that they can't do it themselves. Workers have the knowledge and expertise to make constructive changes, but the union also has to assume a new responsibility."

Jack Bigel reminded the stewards of the role the Union had played by staking its pension fund in helping to pull the city out of the Fiscal Crisis.

The City could not have shed the Fiscal Crisis without us. It was your money that we gambled with, and we gambled with $2.7 billion... That was the resolution of the conflict – the most serious conflict this city ever faced, and we resolved it... There would be no city without what you did, and continue to do.

The conference was a great success. It created a greater sense of togetherness inside Local 831. It allowed Ostrowski and his executive board to strengthen their relationship with the stewards, who were the Union's actual link with each individual Sanitationman. Inside the garage, the steward is the Union. The weekend fired up the stewards and encouraged them to get involved politically, to try and influence all legislation affecting Sanitationmen, and to explain to each individual Sanman what Tier-3 Pensions were, and the need to get rid of them. The stewards headed back to the city that Sunday evening with a better sense of their union's history, where it had come from and where it was headed.

Labor Takes A Nosedive

The times demanded solidarity. As Robert Schrank had pointed out at the first stewards conference, the labor-management picture was changing in 1981. Ronald Reagan had become the 40th President of the United States in spite of the fears – and opposition – of much of organized labor. Those worst fears had come true just one month before the USA's stewards conference. In August 1981, Reagan personally fired 12,000 air traffic controllers who had gone on strike for better conditions. The union that represented them, the Professional Air Traffic Controllers Organization (PATCO) was almost immediately destroyed as a result. Many unions – including PATCO which had supported Reagan for president – were taken off-guard by federal action. "When the unions come out of the shock of what has happened, they are going to have to gird themselves for a very different kind of effort," said Robert Schrank, adding: "Clearly people in the public sector are going to be much more careful about going on strike."

Membership in private-sector unions had already been declining steadily since the peak of union power in the early 1950s. Now, with the President of the United States personally shooting down PATCO, it was open season for unions, especially in private industry.

In order to send a message of solidarity opposed to the new anti-unionism, on September 6, 1981, the AFL-CIO organized the first Labor Day parade in New York City since 1968. Reagan was, of course, not invited, but he tried anyway to crash the party – or at least steal the limelight – by flying in to give Mayor Koch a symbolic check for $85 million toward the Westway, the giant renovation project on New York's West Side.

Reagan was forced to hole up at Gracie Mansion where he was besieged by some of the 4,000 members of PATCO who had come to march in the parade.

Reagan, during his one-day visit, said that "what is good for the American worker is good for America," and spoke of "a new spirit sweeping this country." His unionbusting tactics, particularly in New York State where the Taylor Law hung, as Jack Bigel described it, "hung like the sword of Damocles over the heads of civil servants," exposed Reagan's indifference to the plight of working people, whether in the private or public sector. The spirit Reagan thought was sweeping the country was probably one that Sanmen wanted to swept clear of New York.

All in a Handshake,
or
The Art of Appreciating NYC Sanmen

Amid the doom and gloom of the late 1970s and early 1980s, along came a young woman who wanted to shake the hand of every Sanitationman in

Mierle Laderman Ukeles
Touch Sanitation Performance, 1979-80
"Handshake Ritual" with workers of New York City Department of Sanitation

New York City.

Mierle Ukeles was an artist with an unusual appreciation for municipal workers and, in particular, Sanitationmen. She had developed the radical notion that they needed to be shown a little appreciation and then she set about creating a piece of performance art in order to make that happen.

In this case, the art that she intended to create consisted of the act of shaking the hand of each of the city's 8,000 Sanitationmen and, while doing so, personally speaking a few words of thanks to each man, usually starting with "Thank you for keeping New York City alive."

As she explained at the beginning of her project in 1979:

I'd like to reveal the underlying structure of maintenance that keeps the city going, to make visible the terrible gulf between Sanmen and the public. We're dependent on them, but they feel hated and isolated. We call them garbagemen, but that's assimilating them into the product. If we do that, we have to call ourselves garbage persons. It's our garbage – they don't make it.

At first, many Sanitationmen did not know what to make of this young artist, but word spread quickly – as it always does among these workers of

COURTESY RONALD FELDMAN FINE ARTS, NEW YORK

Mierle Laderman Ukeles
Touch Sanitation Performance, 1984
"Handshake Ritual" with workers of New York City Department of Sanitation

the street – and it was not long before Mierle [pronounced "Marilee"] Ukeles started to be greeted by cries of appreciation and good-humored jibing like "What took you so long?" More than once, a Sanitationman would break down in tears, as years of experiencing only ingratitude for the job melted instantly before this one person's humble show of thanks.

It was a deeply touching tribute to a workforce that had been, for most of its 100-year history, treated as the untouchables of society. It was also ambitious. As of the spring of 1980, Ukeles had been at it for over a year, in every one of the city's 59 districts, in rain and snow and freezing cold, working her art on both day and night shifts, on the streets, in transfer stations and at incinerators, in order to reach every man, and she was still not done.

Art critics, the public and, of course, Sanitationmen and their families applauded. Commissioner Steisel also strongly approved, and designated her Honorary Commissioner of Sanitation. The USA also said its own special thank you to Mierle Ukeles by making her an Honorary Teamster and Member of Local 831.

It is interesting to note that toward the end of her project, Ukeles spoke in a voice that sounded a little less like an artist and a little more like a Sanman. This can be observed in a speech given just two weeks before the end of her project:

As an artist, I have simply tried to get people to see them, to burn an image into the public eye, that this is a human system that keeps New York City alive; that when you throw something out, there is no 'out.' Rather, there's a human being who has to lift it; haul it, get injured because of it, dispose of it; 20,000 tons worth every day.

The Productivity Program – Making Privatization Obsolete?

The result of a different kind of a handshake, the new Productivity Program had saved the city $24 million in just the first two years and one man keeping a tally of that, among other, numbers, was Jack Bigel. It had been Bigel who had engineered the concept of gainsharing and, if $24 million was what the city gained, then he and his staff tried to make sure that Sanmen shared in it.

Even hard-nosed City Councilwoman Carol Bellamy, who had previously pushed hard for privatization, stood up and said, "...I am not prepared to say anything is dead and buried in the ground, but I have to tell you, Jack, from my perspective... if there was a reason for contracting out, I don't see that reason for it anymore."

Bigel, true to habit, was a little ahead of himself. But the essence of his point was clear: if a productivity program worked the way it should, for labor and management, then it made the whole concept of privatization outdated. If effectiveness plus efficiency could be achieved through a productivity program, and the city could retain dedicated civil servants with a sense of public service that "privates" simply do not bring to the job, then privatization could hardly remain an option.

In 1983 Sanman Mario Rossi wrote a poem that may have best summed up the working life – and some of the frustrations – felt by members of Local 831 at that time.

A Sanitationman's Story

When the snow comes down and covers our streets,
If not cleared immediately, the Sanman takes the heat.
When the job is done in record time,
The Sanman is the last to be thanked on a never-ending line.
Yet, the men in forest green work hard each day and night,
To clean our city by the morning's early light.
They work in summer's sun and in the falling snow
Your dedicated Sanman is constantly on the go.
They can't wait for a robbery, or a fire to appear
Because their job is 365 days a year.

The nature of the Sanman's workplace – the street – allows citizens the opportunity for direct communication with the workforce, however brief. There is a political aspect to this sort of exchange that helps explain the power and visibility of the Union. As former Local 831 President Peter Scarlatos described Sanmen: "They're street guys."

The Sanman asks for neither fame nor glory
Just the chance to tell his story.
They fight for what they think is just
Like any hard working family man must.
How much more do they have to do,
In order to be treated like the men in blue?
Twenty-four million, the City saved,
The reward for the Sanman – just Rave! Rave! Rave!
No money for them or their families to spend
Just empty promises with the same old dead end!
The Mayor of the City of New York
Has told the Sanman to take a walk.
Thank you for a job well done
But as for Money, You'll get None!
Promises and accolades will not do,
The Sanman deserves his just due.

Chapter Twelve

Putting Up, Putting Out

"People formed government because they wanted someone to pick up the trash."
- Sanitation Commissioner Brendan Sexton, 1987

The 1980s had gotten off to a bumpy start with the two-man truck, but mid-way through the decade the going got a little smoother. Things were looking up for Local 831. The national recession was giving way to the boom that would earn the Eighties the nickname of "The Greed Decade" and, the Fiscal Crisis of the 1970s was finally spinning itself out. The job looked good to somebody, because in July 1983, more than 100,000 took the test for New York City Sanitationman. Make that "Sanitation worker." As of that test, 83 women passed and entered into the uniformed force – and the Union – for the first time.

The streets of New York were a little cleaner and the forward-looking Norman Steisel was able to think more about what to do with the garbage after it was collected. Steisel's eight years on the job meant he had served longer than any sanitation commissioner since World War II. The USA had often complained about the quick turnover of commissioners. It was hard to establish a relationship with a department where the boss is constantly jumping – or being thrown – overboard. "Your executives live in a revolving door," complained Jack Bigel once during a negotiation session with the city. Harry Nespoli made a similar comment: "You want to build a rapport, but no sooner do you get them broken in, and they're gone. It's frustrating."

Mayor Koch chose Brendan Sexton as the next Commissioner. "People formed government because they wanted someone to pick up the trash," announced Sexton upon being appointed. He added: "City government is where the social contract is realized. It's where the rubber meets the road." It was a bold and progressive statement at a time when the city had difficulty honoring its day-to-day deals, let alone commitments beyond wages and benefits. To top it off, Sexton was the son of a well-known labor leader for the UAW. Michael Bove, the USA's political strategist, recalled: "So you think: 'This guy is good' ...and that's when you know he's not going to last."

Sanitation commissioners came and went. The only question for the union was how their comings and goings might affect the Productivity Program.

A Man Called Schrank

The answer lay no further away than Robert Schrank. Appointed the first Chairman of the Tripartite Panel in 1980, Schrank's fifteen years in that capacity saw him through the Koch, Dinkins and into the Giuliani administration. His long tenure as chairman allowed him to ease the Productivity Program through its stormy beginnings and also helped the young program weather changes in mayors and their staffs.

Robert "Bob" Schrank was no ordinary public administrator. He was, as he put it, "from the world of work." He had started his working days during the Depression as a plumber, then mechanic, and eventually machinist. Along the way, he became a labor organizer. In the 1960s, he ran a City agency for youth employment until he was tapped by John Lindsay to become Deputy Director of Manpower. Schrank continued to pursue his education and wound up with a PhD in Sociology. An expert in worker motivation and labor-management relations, Schrank served as consultant to major corporations around the world, from General Motors to General Electric.

By 1980, when Robert Schrank spoke, management listened. It was a time when workers had increasing expectations regarding job satisfaction and security, but were finding less of those things as the Reagan administration continued to let down labor. Studies showed that more Americans were dissatisfied with their work than ever. Schrank's approach to solving this problem involved solutions that ranged from refreshing to radical, given the attitudes of management at the time. To counter boredom on the job, for example, Schrank suggested that employers look at the overall quality of work life: "...I tell employers that they should expand social life at the plant to increase productivity."

Schrank advocated any reasonable means, even "schmoozing" in the work place, in order to keep employee morale up. He did not see problems in black and white so much as in shades of gray. "Job dissatisfaction is not a condition. It's not a steady state, but rather, an experience. Some [workers] are very disaffected on Monday, but by the time Friday rolls around the job isn't so bad."

Schrank was just as tough on labor. But his focus in both situations was always centered on the needs of human beings first, and workers and bosses, second. With his blue-collar background and acquired credentials as a consultant to management, Schrank turned out to be the perfect candidate to chair man of the Tripartite Panel.

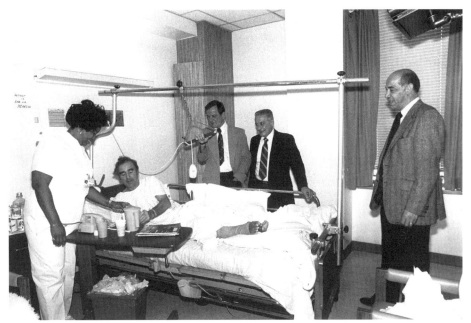

Eddie Ostrowski, Val Pappa and Jimmy Alongi pay a visit to an injured Sanitation-man in the hospital. This sort of support for workers is an important part of the job for Union executives.

Schrank remained a mechanic at heart and applied a nuts-and-bolts approach to problem solving. Confronted with a problem, some bureaucrats bury themselves deeper in the paper cocoons of their offices. Schrank would do just the opposite and head straight for the factory floor. In his new role as Tripartite chairman, he did the equivalent and hit the streets. As Schrank described it, "You needed to physicalize and go out and ride with the trucks, with the guys... to get a sense of the job."

So Schrank got in his car and followed sanitation crews around in order to resolve situations where workers were getting docked. Unlike members of the "Rat Squad," Schrank's motivation was not to entrap Sanitation Workers in petty violations, but to get to the root of the problem. For him, the only way to do that was observe it with his own eyes. Right and wrong for Schrank did not revolve around workers' breaks running an extra five minutes over, but instead was based on the goals of the Productivity Program being achieved in a reasonable manner. Schrank put it this way: "My feeling about docks was that it needed to be gross negligence."

Schrank's hands-on approach and fair judgment made fans of both the Department and the union. Allen Brawer calls Schrank "an extraordinary human being... a guy who could get above the day-to-day stuff and could see the bigger picture. He even brought a sense of fun, a sense of 'change is fun'

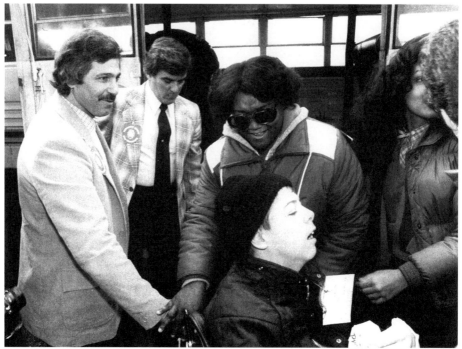

Harry Nespoli clasping hands with a Union sister.

with him. Coming when he did, at the beginning of the program, he helped define not just the role of the chairman and the Tripartite Panel, but the whole Productivity Program."

At the Third Stewards Conference in 1983, Schrank related the need for people to talk to each other as a factor in the successful introduction of the two-man truck.

The general experience in industry in the last 5 to 10 years has been more and more to get input from the people who use the equipment. There was this great discovery made about 10 years ago that people who work with equipment actually might know something about it. And, of course, it hasn't been bad for me because I'll tell you a secret. As a consultant I have done very well... primarily because employers, or "bosses" as you might know them, never talk to employees.

Schrank closed his speech by touching on one of his favorite themes: the need for unions to change and re-invent themselves with both new thinking and new leadership. It carried a special message to Local 831, which at that time was infused with the transitional shift to Eddie Ostrowski and the next

160

generation of younger leaders headed up by Scarlatos and Nespoli.

Institutions that can change and can be flexible and come up with new ways of working, I believe, are the ones that are going to survive. Institutions that simply lay back and say, you know the way we did it a hundred, twenty-five years ago, or ten years ago, or last year is the only thing we understand, I believe, are going to have serious problems.

I think in the leadership of your union and the people who have worked for you, you've shown an enormous ability to be flexible and to accept new ideas and to figure out how to make them work... What I would say to you is keep that ball bouncing... But make sure the changes occur, that you're on top of it in terms of what is the best way to do the job, what's in the best interest of your membership and what's the best way to make it a better job and a better place to work.

Schrank later recalled the Productivity Program as "the perfect fit, the right plan at the right time. It allowed the Department to act in its own self-interest and it also served to remind the Department of the value of its workers. For the Union, it allowed the involvement of workers in all matters affecting them." As he described it, "the incentive was necessary for productivity and anyway that was the deal with the Financial Control Board still keeping an eye on City spending – you had to show productivity in order to substantiate any wage increases."

Days of Mayor David Dinkins

In 1989 David Dinkins was elected mayor of New York City. It was at this time that recycling was introduced. Both met with mixed results.

As of the time David Dinkins took office, the Productivity Program had almost ten years under its belt. It had become a hard asset for the Uniformed Sanitationmen's Association as the Union continued to negotiate better contracts, fight for the elimination of Tier 3 and then Tier 4 pensions, and try and prevent more layoffs.

Dinkins faced an uphill battle from the start. Battling the biggest budget deficit in ten years. Dinkins, while still shaking hands with labor leaders, got off on the wrong foot with them. The new Mayor's budget actions also drew criticism from the watchdog group, the Citizens Budget Commission.

Less than a year later, in November 1990, Sanitation Workers staged a slowdown in order to protest the announced layoff of 600 workers as well as the old familiar problem of a contract that had expired the previous June. Commissioner Steve Polan did not stop there and indicated that even more cuts might be coming in 1991.

Local 831 was forced to draw a line in the sand. Eddie Ostrowski remarked, "It will drain the energy and enthusiasm of Sanitation Workers who have provided New York City hundreds of millions in productivity savings over the last decade, only to turn around and see their ranks slashed at the first sign of trouble." By the following June, the City had delivered 6,000 layoff notices to municipal workers, with 940 DSNY employees among them. A total of 600 Uniformed Sanitation Workers lost their jobs.

"I've got babies, man," Sanitation Worker Gregory Vann told a reporter after finding out that his name was "on the list" of san workers to be laid off. He added: "You never had a little kid come to you and say, 'I'm hungry.'"

Union leaders, led by Eddie Ostrowski, denounced Dinkins "doomsday budget" that included plans to close libraries and turn off street lights. Speaking to the press, Ostrowski expressed his outrage.

My first concern, of course, is for every man and woman who has been laid off, in the Sanitation Department and elsewhere. This is a human tragedy that will be lived daily by hundreds of my members and thousands of other city workers trying to pay bills and provided for their families

The city administration is going to learn quickly that sanitation services, just like police and fire services, are essential to the health and well-being of our citizens. When the streets start piling up with litter and garbage, it will reinforce everyone's notion that New York City is no longer a good place to live or work.

Reacting to the layoffs, Sanitation Workers worked according to contract. The Union, of course, disavowed any connection with it, in spite of Commissioner Polan's comments that the observation that it was "very well organized."

As punishment for the slowdown, the Department filed disciplinary charges against 600 Sanitation Workers. Polan stepped in, however, and credited the Union with getting the workers back up to speed quickly. He then had almost all of the charges.

In the meantime, the Union got to work immediately on efforts to get its laid-off members rehired. It also provided some temporary financial support.

Recycling – When More is Less

Neither the citizens nor the Department of Sanitation seemed ready for recycling.

According to the Department, the new recycling program got very limited cooperation from city's residents. Things didn't go so well as expected for the new recycling program. City residents separated only half the materials that they could have. Commissoner Stephen Polan tried to wake up the City with comments like "New Yorkers have to face up to the fact that there is no free lunch in terms of waste disposal."

The leadership of Local 831 made sure that lunch was not going to be on them.

Contrary to some accounts, Sanitation Workers were receptive to the new recycling program. Their Productivity Program was once again poised to make recycling into the same quantifiable and efficient operation as garbage collection. Recycling posed many new problems in terms of equipment, manpower, allotting and timing coverage in different districts, but the Union was ready to deal with it.

The City, however, was not. There were too many unknowns and the Department was unable to present clear options to the union. This lack of agreement between the Union and the Department – in addition to the weak attempt to recycle on the part of the citizens – spelled problems. And so recycling under David Dinkins never really got off the ground.

.

● ● ● ● ●

The arrival of the two-man truck in the early 1980s may have signaled the beginning of the Productivity Program, but it took another dozen years, however, before the program really went into action.

In the meantime, it was eyed with suspicion by some, and with envy by others. No one was certain exactly how Rudy Giuliani viewed it, but the Mayor-elect's promise to "reinvent government" did not sound like it boded well for anyone or department in general. Giuliani cracked a sly smile when he announced: "There are no sacred cows."

No one knew how much of it was pure rhetoric or whether Giuliani, in fact, was going to make good on his promise to cut 30,000 city jobs, amounting to 14% of the city work force. The USA, in particular, was rattled over Giuliani's threats to privatize sanitation. A man with a mission, the Mayor-elect had carved out a serious reputation as an aggressive U.S. This, plus the overwhelming consensus that the Dinkins administration had done little by way of productivity except to extend sanitation routes, helped set the stage for what was shaping up to be the battle of the 1990s.

Chapter Thirteen

Two-fisted Productivity

"Productivity isn't everything, but in the end it's almost everything."
- economist Paul Krugman, 1989

"That smell pays my mortgage."
- Bill Corcoran, Sanitationman, 1994

Local 831 had much at stake with the Productivity Program. The risk was great, but so was the payback, if everybody – labor and management – did what they were supposed to. As for the Union's rank and file, motivation pivoted off the program's system of performance-based rewards and penalties. For its part, the Department looks for its own sort of reward from productivity – a savings of hundreds of millions of dollars to the city.

In the last 25 years, the city has gained over $2 billion in savings due to the Productivity Program. The program's mechanism of gainsharing allows part of those gains to be shared by the worker. If, on the other hand, those goals are not met, then the worker is penalized and docked that bonus. The city is also penalized, in the sense that it has lost the potential productivity savings. With the Productivity Program, labor and management sink or swim together. It becomes in the vested interest of both to make sure the program succeeds, and that "docks" are kept to a minimum.

When problems arise, both individual performance and program performance are looked at. In an interview in 2006, Alton Marshall, then in his twelfth year as chairman of the Tripartite Panel that oversees the Productivity Program, described the interrelationship between Sanitation Workers and management:

If I see that the guys on the street are having the same problem

over and over again... say, getting docked for the same thing repeatedly... that does not mean to me that they are necessarily screwing up. It could be the opposite – that there's a problem with management and the docks are just the symptom of something that needs to get fixed on the other end.

New Blood

Eddie Ostrowski retired in 1993. His presidency had served as the transition from the USA's stormy beginnings to a union now headed calmly for the next century.

His term had also seen productivity rise to the forefront of issues between the Union and the City. The savings – over $1 billion in the first 12 years alone – were greater than anyone had predicted. The gainsharing allowed Sanmen's wages – with overtime and shift differentials – to surpass those of both fire and police for the first time. Both sides – labor and management –were sold on the program.

Peter Scarlatos became the third president of Local 831. He had been groomed to take over for nearly ten years and was now backed up by Harry Nespoli in the V.P. slot. The rank and file made it official by an overwhelming vote. It was a new and younger generation of leadership. More importantly, Scarlatos and Nespoli were a team that had cut their teeth on the new the Productivity Program.

Another major influence on the thinking of Scarlatos and Nespoli was exercised by Jack Bigel, who had served as mentor to the two men since the beginning of their involvement in the Union leadership. Now in his eighties, Bigel did not limit himself to the role of older wise man, and continued to show the feistiness he was famous for. "Jack was a southpaw," recalls Bigel's longtime associate, Allen Brawer. "That meant that even while he was shaking hands with his right, he was ready with his left."

Always the revolutionary, Bigel set the tone for the new era with the slogan: "Productivity happens from the bottom up." The Uniformed Sanitationmen's Association knew something about starting at the bottom from its own history. So the Union readily passed the concept along to its rank and file, always letting Sanitation Workers know that, while productivity started at the bottom, everything from there could only be up.

Scarlatos, Nespoli and Bigel. It was a dynamic trio, and they would need every bit of their combined intelligence and union experience to deal with the new mayor of New York.

It was a chilly day for labor when Rudolph Giuliani took office in January 1994. The USA leadership girded themselves for an ugly battle. What they got instead was something different: Randy Levine.

A young labor lawyer and Giuliani's pick for Labor Commissioner, Levine was that rarest of species: a man who knew law, who knew the city, and who respected blue collar workers. Since labor relations with City Hall had, at times in the past, resembled a political circus, Levine immediately made it clear that it was not going to be "business as usual" at City Hall. In getting things off to a fresh start, he said, "I'd like to sit down with labor leaders and hear their side of the story." It was an unusual and refreshing approach for a highly-appointed City official and it marked the beginning of a relationship that is, as Levine puts it, "like a marriage, built on mutual respect." Recalling the change in approach, Harry Nespoli comments:

Levine listened. The City was starting to take the Productivity Program seriously... and it was looking like we could finally get to a place where management and labor could join forces...

An Idea whose Time had Come

Levine was open to incentives for workers, as well as greater union input into management. It became clear quickly that he was interested in creating an environment that was going to allow the Productivity Program to grow to maturity. "Randy Levine was one of the few men on the city side that Jack Bigel ever respected and trusted completely," remembers Allen Brawer.

Levine, who today is President of the New York Yankees, an organization noted for its own kind of productivity, looks back and comments:

When I came in, there was a serious budget situation... productivity was a major issue. The talk ranged from reinventing government to privatizing. As for the Sanitation Workers, I honestly felt they had been maligned. My feeling was that they worked hard and were not overpaid. At the same time, we needed to get control of the budget and it seemed like productivity was one of the best ways to do it. Local 831 was the right union to be doing it with. Many times they had ideas that were better than ours.

Three Contracts Crank up Productivity

The Union, which had been without a contract for 27 months when Giuliani came into office, took advantage of the positive atmosphere and charged ahead in its negotiations. By August 1994, the two sides reached a new agreement. It was the first of three contracts over a 10-year period from 1992-2002 that ratcheted up the Productivity Program to the next level. Each of the three contracts pivoted off increased productivity standards.

Labor-Management Gets its Second Wind

About the time that the Giuliani administration had its first year under its belt, in late 1994, the Productivity Program got its own boost with the appointment of Alton Marshall as the new chairman of the Tripartite Panel. Up to that point, Marshall's main interaction with Sanitation Workers had been during the Sanitationmen's Strike of 1968, when he served Nelson A. Rockefeller as Chief-of-Staff. A former Marine and veteran of the Battle of Iwo Jima, Marshall was known as a no-nonsense, fair-minded public administrator whose career reached back over five decades. Jack Bigel knew Marshall and supported his appointment to the panel, telling Local 831: "He may not help us, but he won't kill us."

Marshall's experience and impartiality consistently served to strengthen the Productivity Program during the implementation of these three contracts. Just as both sides – labor and management – had a stake in the Productivity Program, it can be said that each new contract raised the stakes considerably higher. Marshall comments on his role as chairman:

Any productivity standard against which a worker would be measured and paid – or penalized – for their performance... is a good thing. The Tripartite Panel keeps an eye on getting the right kind of work done for the right kind of action or improvement. If labor-management breaks down, you have to have someplace to go... Once a thing has been quantified, it takes away management's ability to say "Do this – Do that" without a reason.

Allen Brawer underlines the importance of the Tripartite Panel and its chairman: "the chairman is king, his decision is binding, and it can't be appealed. The panel adds value in a lot of ways. When the numbers call the shots, and the Chairman makes a decision that is not popular with the Union, then he takes the heat for it instead of the [union] president... and it work boths ways with labor and management... so long as decisions are impartial, the panel adds tremendous value to the Productivity Program."

How the Program Empowers the Rank and File

The Tripartite Panel Chairman has contributed to this sense of empowerment in a very important way: by setting precedents that turn on issues of what is right for the successful performance of the job. Marshall, in two key decisions, expanded the jurisdiction of the Panel to ensure that workers were given a fair shake, and that the Department could not use its power or discipline to undermine the Productivity Program. As labor lawyer and Local 831 consultant Alan Klinger observed: "Marshall, coming from state government, knew how easily management could disaffect the workforce and for that reason he worked hard to foster true labor-management cooperation."

While the Department weighs productivity in a literal sense, the Tripartite

Workers remove litter and debris after a Yankees World Series victory. Cleanup details after such special events is just one of a myriad number of jobs for Sanitation Workers.

Panel uses a set of scales calibrated more to overall productivity – and a larger sense of justice. Marshall's sense of fairness tapped into the essential energy that is the core of the rank and file: the individual worker, linked with fellow workers, is the Union. All for one, and one for all. In this way, solidarity and sense of family has been reawakened through the Productivity Program.

Input, Output, Never Staying Put

The Union, as only one of three members of the Tripartite Panel, has to line up its facts and make its case in the strongest possible terms. Each case that comes before the Panel assumes importance on two levels: 1) because an immediate and specific problem needs to be resolved for the sake of the individual workers concerned; and 2) because each decision may become part of the larger body of precedents that sets future policy and will, therefore, affect all workers for years to come.

The Productivity Program allows the union leadership to get involved in every work issue that affects productivity. Those include allocation of people and equipment, routing and districting, and time management. Also, because every single thing affects productivity, there is another parallel to the theme of 'all for one, and one for all': that the Productivity Program allows the Union to have input into every aspect of the running of the Department. The significance of this is commented on by Allen Brawer:

> **Management can always say, "Do it anyway." That's their right, though it won't get them the results they want. The Productivity Program allows the City to see the virtue of cooperation – that incentives are the difference and that, in the end, the way to get more out of your workforce is by letting them have more say over matters that affect them.**

> **In the rest of America, management pushes the standards. Here instead, you have a union pushing the standards – with amazing results.**

Some Sanitation Workers might have remembered that, during his visit to Local 831's Union Hall in 1996, the Mayor said: "You provide public safety in ways that sometimes aren't focused on." Giuliani was, of course, referring to the hundreds of situations that had taken place over the course of the 20th century where Streetcleaners and Sanitation Workers had saved lives and helped protect the citizenry by intervening in fires and crimes while on duty clearing the streets of the city.

Chapter Fourteen

831 Today: Men, Women, Workers, Heroes

"I bet you could find statistics that say that being a Sanitation Worker in this day and age is more dangerous than being a policeman or fireman."
- Michael Bloomberg, campaigning for Mayor

During his mayoral campaign, Michael Bloomberg took a lot of flack for comparing the dangers of being a Sanitation Worker to those of a cop or firefighter.

Mayor Bloomberg was merely citing studies showing that Sanitation Workers have an average life expectancy four years lower than police or firefighters. That depressing statistic is arrived at not just as a result of the physical accidents – mechanical and vehicular – that take their toll; Sanitation Workers also suffer from the long-term effects of handling hazardous waste and noxious chemicals constantly, day in, day out.

Perhaps it is because of his outspokenness on their behalf that the City's Sanitation Workers appreciate Mike Bloomberg. Or perhaps it's just because the Mayor, who's famous for working his staff hard, values the practical results – and savings to the city from productivity – of the job that Sanmen do. "The city works because of them," summed up Bloomberg in an hour-long interview for this Union history.

More than any other New York City mayor, Bloomberg has brought to City Hall the sensibility of a private businessman who values employees as assets, not liabilities. Bloomberg likes to refer to himself as the "CEO of the city" and views dedicated civil servants as "talent" that must be rewarded. And, again to the benefit of Sanitation Workers, he understands productivity better than almost anybody and knows that is the key to cleaning the streets. And keeping the streets clean, and clear of crime, are two of the essential ingredients to the "selling" of New York.

Mayor Michael Bloomberg receives the endorsement of Local 831 in one of his many visits to the Union Hall.

"I'm not smarter than anybody else, but I'll outwork them," says Bloomberg with a smile. It's that kind of modesty and his self-deprecating sense of humor that make it easy for him to have a conversation with workers who perform physical labor for a living. It has also helped him hold a conversation, in fact, many conversations with Local 831 which he describes as "possibly the best disciplined Union in the city." In the same breath he calls Harry Nespoli "as good a labor leader, honest and flexible, as I've met." The mayor goes on to quip: "The only other person who delivers more than Harry Nespoli is Mariano Rivera."

Bloomberg also pinpoints the benefits provided by a comprehensive and intelligent public approach to sanitation:

> **I look at private versus public and the difference is the civil servant. If you treat them with respect and you're clear as to what you expect of them... that's the key. We've got the best sanitation services in the world, the streets are cleaner now than in recorded history. In the past we've tried to see if private carters could do it more efficiently, but I believe that certain services – and sanitation is at the top of the list – should simply be performed by the city in order to have maximum control over them. That control is the key to keeping the city safe.**

James F. Hanley is the Commissioner of Labor Relations and has had many opportunities to witness Bloomberg's ability to communicate effectively with municipal unions, including Local 831. "The Mayor is a businessman... Koch, Dinkins, Giuliani, Bloomberg, they're all into good government, but Bloomberg... he's into productivity."

Before Hanley joined the ranks of civil service, he worked as an electrician. Today, there's still something hands-on about his approach to labor negotiations. He has been described as "tough" and "tenacious," but he is quick to praise the "fantastic leadership" of Local 831. Hanley explains:

Some unions were more concerned about what the other guy [union] got. It's a historical relationship that goes back to 1898. But the Sanitation Union was always pragmatic, negotiating from its strength...from productivity. And in other matters, the Tripartite panel allows them and us to move on to the next issue. It's a system that works, so we don't get bogged down. Almost everything is resolved at the table... Things tend not to fester.

Hanley's job gives him a one-of-a kind perspective from which to comment on another unique – and almost unquantifiable – value provided by the city's Sanitation Workers: public service beyond the call of duty. For more than a hundred years, and well before even 1898, Street Cleaners and Sanitation Workers have on innumerable occasions stepped into dangerous situations and risked their own lives to save those of their fellow citizens. There are hundreds of reported instances where they have run into burning buildings to rescue those in peril, jumped into rivers to save someone from drowning, stopped muggings and sometimes pursued and apprehended the muggers, and often simply provided emergency care for a citizen in distress.

One of the more notable such acts of bravery took place in September 2005 in the East Flatbush section of Brooklyn. Damon Allen and his partner, Michael Kalinowski, were working their shift at 4 a.m. when they saw smoke coming out of a building. They instantly headed for the fire. Nearing the building, they observed a man holding a baby on the third-floor fire escape. "Help, catch my baby!" They positioned themselves below and Allen shouted instructions to the man, Damon Whyte, who then let his four-year old baby drop safely into Allen's arms.

Sanitation Workers, men and women, have distinct advantages that enable them to perform these acts: they are, in essence, already and almost constantly deployed on the street; they are physically strong and capable; and, they are always, in their own way, on the lookout for action. No other action ever required more of their public spirited service than the catastrophe that took place on Sept. 11, 2001.

Rescue Girl From Fire

Life-Saving Pickup By Rookie Sanmen

By REUVEN BLAU

Sanitation Workers Michael Kalinowski and Damon Allen were in the middle of their Sept. 14 shift when they saw smoke billowing out of a first-floor window of an East Flatbush building at 4 a.m.

'Catch My Baby'

They drove up to the three-story apartment complex to check out the situation. "When we got there, every-body was running out of the building," Mr. Allen said in a phone interview that evening.

"We heard people calling for help, so we tried to help anyone in any way we could," Mr. Kalinowski added.

The two men noticed a man holding a young girl trapped on the third-floor fire escape and screaming, "Help, catch my baby."

With flames engulfing the

(Continued on Page 11)

The Chief-Leader/Adrienne Haywood-James

IN GOOD HANDS: Sanitation Worker Damon Allen helped save a life when he caught a 4-year-old girl whose step-father tossed her from his third-floor fire escape as they tried to flee a blaze in their building.

LOCAL 831 ARCHIVES

Harry Nespoli checks in as the results of a Union election are about to be announced.

Sanitation Workers and the Cleanup After 9-11

"They are the unsung heroes," announces Jim Hanley in describing the role that the city's Sanitation Workers played in the rescue and cleanup operations after the the World Trade Center disaster. "It was a horrific scene, and Sanworkers tirelessly, quietly and continually worked... every single day. They don't normally get the same accolades as others, the cameras don't usually show them."

In addressing a meeting of Local 831 members shortly after 9-11, Mayor Rudy Giuliani expressed the same sentiment in his own words: "You provide public safety in ways that sometimes aren't focused on."

Using everything from their bare hands to front-end loaders, Sanitation Workers paid scant attention to their own welfare in order to help with the search for victims in the immediate aftermath. They continued to work at the site for long shifts and round the clock for more than two months, amid the still smoldering remains and noxious gases. By the time the job of cleaning up was finally done, the equivalent of 90,000 truckloads of debris had been

175

Sanitation Commissioner John Doherty (left) and Union President Harry Nespoli (right) team up on gridiron strategies at an outing of DSNY's football team, "Strongest."

removed.

First Deputy Commissioner Michael Bimonte describes the cleanup after 9-11 as "one of the shining examples of the Union and the Department coming together for the public good. Any emergency today, no matter what in the city, and Sanitation Workers will be there, doing what they can to help."

The Union in a New Century

Harry Nespoli has worked full-throttle since taking over as president of the USA in 2002. The beginning of his term was marked by the layoff of 515 Sanitation Workers in April 2003. By June, 200 had been hired back.

In 2004, the Union won another victory with the passage of the "Heart Bill" that made it easier for Sanitation Workers to identify that the increasing incidence of heart problems they suffer are related to the job. The law presumes that heart disease resulting in death or disability is job-related and grants benefits to workers or their families.

Some of the problems that Nespoli has had to face almost seem trivial, as in the case of Departmental dress codes. In December 2002, First Deputy Commissioner Peter Montalbano put out an order that read:

As a quasi-military uniform force, certain standards of personal

Attorney Alan Klinger discusses some of the legal ramifications of the proposed contract.

appearance and grooming must be established for all uniform personnel of the department.

Two male Sanitation Workers were sent home for a day without pay when they refused to remove their hooped earrings after being ordered to do so by a supervisor. The Department threatened to keep the workers suspended, but the union filed a complaint. In the end, the two men were allowed to return to work provided they covered their earrings. Interviewed by the Times, Nespoli criticized the Department:

The boss is going to come out with a ruler and measure our guys' fingernails? Give me a break! Next they'll hire a beautician to come in and fix up the guys. I don't know who's getting bored down there, that they're sitting down and talking about body piercing.

In 2004 Nespoli scored another victory when Governor Pataki signed a bill that permitted Sanitation Workers to live outside the city in the nearby suburban counties. The union had lobbied for the measure for over twenty years. Nespoli commented to the civil service newspaper, The Chief: "This

NEW YORK DAILY NEWS

The funeral of Eva Barrientos, the first woman Sanitation Worker to die as a result of injuries on the job.

is very important to my members. What good is staying in the city if you can't buy a home?" Regarding the near impossibility of a Sanitation Worker being able to afford a home in one of the city's five boroughs, Nespoli added: "Nobody can dispute the fact that the real-estate market has exploded to the point where the average worker can't afford it."

Tragedy has also visited the Union during Nespoli's watch. A 36-year veteran of the force, the USA president is no stranger to the job-related deaths and disabilities suffered by Sanitation Workers. Sadly, in 2004, the first accidental death of a female Sanitation Worker took place when 41-year old Eva Barrientos, a mother of three, was killed on the job. She had climbed to the top of a garbage truck in order to free up a trash bag that had jammed the compactor. While attempting this, a mechanical lever came down on her and killed her.

They did not stop there. In 2005, Local 831 negotiated what the New York Times called "the best contract for any municipal union in the current round contract renewals with the city." This new contract gave to Sanitation Workers, for the first time in the city's history, a starting salary to rival that of police. It was in the spring of 1972 that then USA president John J. DeLury said "I see no reason that Sanitationmen should not make the same salary as the police." Finally, thirty-three years later, that and more had come to pass.

Consultant Allen Brawer gives a presentation on the relative merits of different Union contract proposals to Local 831's Bargaining Committee.

This did not happen by accident. In its 2005 collective bargaining sessions with the City, Local 831 was neither aiming for pure wage increases nor seeking to overtake the other uniformed services in starting salary. Instead, both sides negotiated a contract that continued to build on the twenty-five year commitment to the Productivity Program. Just as that program had been constantly improved and fine-tuned in increments, so had the wages and benefits of Sanitationmen. There was no doubt as to the chief benefit that had accrued to the city: over $2 billion in manpower savings achieved over that quarter-century. The higher wages of Sanitation Workers, combined with these savings to the city, could mean only one thing. The Productivity Program was here to stay.

Union as Family

"What is the epitome of a good work situation? When working here is like working in a big family."
- Robert Schrank, management consultant

For all the talk of wages and benefits that have flowed from the Productivity

Program for the rank and file of Local 831, the importance of teamwork and partnership cannot be overstated. Working through labor-management problems with the Department is both a challenge for the Union, and its own reward.

Sanitation Commissioner John Doherty described it in 2009 like this: "We work together, the Department and the Union. We have to. Of course we're always going to want more, but that's why the Union is there... they're going to protect their members and we are going to work with them. The Productivity Program has made everybody a winner."

Even at the highest levels of the Department, there is an acceptance of the Union as the fabric holding the workforce together. The partnership that has been put in place through labor/management meetings between the Union and the Department adds another level of rapport. The constant communication within and from the Union result in a healthy give and take that has helped make the productivity program a win-win for both sides.

Cleaning, not collecting, is the essential job of New York's Strongest. Cleaning the streets, collecting the garbage, and removing the snow all work toward one aim: clearing the way for a city on the move. The job could be likened to that of clearing the tracks for a great train coming, or of clearing the runway for an enormous aircraft taking off. Those descriptions, however, do not capture the rhythm and daily beat that Sanitation Workers contribute to the pulse of the city. There is a nurturing aspect to what Sanitation Workers do and, in that sense, it is not unlike the farmer who must clear the land before sowing it; so that the fields will be their most productive; so that both the land, and the living things on it, will be fruitful and multiply. It is in that clearing that a home, a family, a city, and a Union, are built.

Chapter Fifteen

Memphis, New York and Martin Luther King, Jr.

"We wanted to recognize Dr. King's contributions to racial equality and labor justice – in particular his relationship to the working men and women of America."
- Harry Nespoli

Sanmen in New York had been trying for years to get Martin Luther King Day as a holiday. In 2008, the Uniformed Sanitationmen's Association finally achieved this goal. On January 17, 2008, in one of the most public and important events ever, Local 831 celebrated that fact and commemorated the life of the slain civil rights leader. Sanitation Workers had succeeded in becoming the first and, to date, the only uniformed force in the city to negotiate Dr. King's birthday as a paid holiday.

On that day, Nespoli led a parade of four-hundred Sanitation Workers marching side-by-side from USA headquarters on Cliff Street, west along Broadway to New York City's oldest house of worship, Trinity Church. The church was packed with representatives from every municipal union as well as state and city political figures including Mayor Bloomberg and former Mayor David Dinkins.

One of the participants invited by Local 831 to speak on January 17, 2008 at Trinity Church was Jesse Epps, a veteran labor organizer who was personally involved with the Memphis strike and who was with Dr. King when he died. How he came to be invited to the Jan. 17, 2008 function is a story of how King's influence spanned two cities and two unions at different ends of the country, and nearly at the same time.

A Tale of Two Unions

Martin Luther King, Jr. was assassinated on April 4, 1968 while supporting a strike by Sanitation Workers in Memphis, Tennessee. What was not known – and only came to light in the course of Local 831 researching its own history – was the relationship of the strike in Memphis to the 1968 New York City Sanitation Workers's strike.

Both strikes took place in February. As Chapter 6 of this book describes, the first took place in New York City and lasted nine days, from Friday, February 2nd until Saturday, February 10th, burying the city – and Mayor John Lindsay along with it – in garbage. The second strike began in Memphis, Tennessee, two days later, on Monday, February 12, "taking its cue from New York," according to the Times.

Further proof of the influence of the New York Strike was provided by Memphis Mayor Henry Loeb who told his city's Sanitation Workers "This isn't New York!" and flatly told them "Go back to work!" They stood fast.

The Memphis strike soon became known as the "I Am A Man" strike, as the workers universally adopted the slogan, "I am a man," and carried signs proclaiming it. Memphis Sanitation Union president Taylor Rogers explained the special significance of the phrase: "What that meant, 'I am man,' is we would have no more of being called 'boy.' We had been called boy for a hundred years or more and now we were saying that we weren't going to be called that anymore: we are men. I am a man." Similarities to Italians in New York City 100 years ago could be made.

In all, Martin Luther King made three trips to Memphis in order to lend his support to the striking Sanitation Workers. During his involvement in the strike, Dr. King saw and spoke about the essential value of all human labor and the role of all workers – including Sanitation Workers – in holding our society together. Martin Luther King knew that this "value" was not about dollars and cents, but about basic human worth and dignity – the essence of the labor movement.

In March 1968, with the strike already five weeks old, King traveled twice to Memphis. He did not seek to become embroiled in what had started as a local labor action, but King's first visit on March 18 made a very strong impression on him. He soon saw what became known as the "I Am A Man Strike" as a deep symbol of the fate of poor working people throughout the country. As the strike wore into its second month, King's advent incited new energy, higher stakes – and growing threats from white racists.

On March 28, Dr. King walked with strikers and their supporters in a march turned bloody when police unleashed mace, clubs and guns, arresting hundreds, injuring more than sixty, and shooting three including a sixteen-year old boy who died on the spot from shotgun wounds.

Disheartened, but determined to hold to his doctrine of non-violence, King organized a second march to take place six days later. He then returned to Memphis on April 3 – his third visit in three weeks in support of the strike

182

Local 831 travels to Memphis to meet with veterans of the 1968 "I Am A Man Strike." Seated are Taylor Rogers, right, and Joe Warren, strikers. Next to Harry are St. John Middleton, left, and Ronald Prattis.

– and that evening delivered his famous "From The Mountaintop" speech in which he asked that the focus remain on the cause of the Sanitation Workers and not on the violence of the previous week. He also eerily foretold of his impending death on what turned out to be the eve of his assassination.

King was murdered the next day, on April 4, 1968, just as he stepped onto the balcony of the Lorraine Motel on his way to another rally of Sanitation Workers. The accuracy of Martin Luther King's prediction the night before – and the resulting shockwaves that his death sent throughout the country – have long overshadowed the focus on the plight of the Sanitation Workers of Memphis, then or now.

Local 831 Travels to Memphis

Nearly forty years later, on November 29, 2007, President Harry Nespoli stood just a few steps from that very spot on the balcony of the Lorraine Motel. After learning of the possible connection between the two strikes, Nespoli had quickly decided to do a little research himself, but not of the book-variety. A man who believes more in action than words, it was only natural for him to immediately book a flight to Memphis in order to meet

Memphis Press-Scimitar

A Scripps-Howard Newspaper

CHARLES H. SCHNEIDER   W. FRANK AYCOCK JR.
Editor   *Business Manager*

Telephone: 526-2141; Want Ads, 526-8892; Circulation, 525-7801
Address: 495 Union Avenue, Memphis, Tenn., 38101

Page 6   Monday, February 12, 1968

Give Light and the People Will Find Their Own Way

Garbage Mess – N.Y. and Here

The country has been astonished at the garbage mess in New York, but it might have known that the trouble there was catching—as M e m p h i s learned today when about half our 1,300 Sanitation Department workers refused to go to work on the 7 a.m. shift.

Memphis Public Works officials said flatly the strike here was triggered by the developments which brought the New York strikers pay increases.

Memphis sanitation workers seek an increase in top pay for laborers from $1.80 to $2.40 an hour and a boost for crew chiefs from $2.10 to $3 per hour, both by July 1.

It is to be fervently hoped that the Memphis trouble will be settled before it becomes comparable to that in New York.

The New York strikers violated a law that bans strikes by public employes. Memphis Public Works officials say they believe the Memphis strike violates a ruling by Special Chancellor William B. Rosenfield in 1966 that Public Works employes did not have a right to strike or picket the city.

★ ★ ★

Meanwhile, in New York, garbage collectors and other city workers were moving the huge piles of odorous, rat-infested garbage after a set-to between Mayor Lindsay and Governor Nelson Rockefeller.

The city agreed to a wage settlement comparable to pay raises given other city employes. The union rejected them.

When Mayor Lindsay asked the governor to call out the National Guard to clean up the garbage accumulation, other unions threatened a general strike and the

governor refused. Then Rockefeller set up his own "mediation" panel which promptly recommended a higher pay raise for the strikers which Lindsay promptly rejected.

Next, Rockefeller said he would ask the Legislature to approve the state taking over the New York sanitation department, and bill the city for the cost. However, last night he said he would give Lindsay three days to work out a settlement with the union. He said he would ask the Legislature today to approve the take-over, but hold it in abeyance three days.

So nothing really has been settled, New York's so-called anti-strike law has been splintered and the city's 8,000,000 residents once again bullied and endangered by union muscle.

This mess augurs more trouble ahead, both in New York and in other cities where garbage collectors and other city employes are watching the New York developments.

The important principle in New York, Memphis and everywhere is that public employes have no moral right to strike against the public, whether present law forbids it or not.

Though the g a r b a g e controversies dramatize this principle because the public health is involved, it holds good for all public employes.

This puts a special responsibility on public officials to see that governmental employes get a fair deal, but it does not relieve the workers and their leaders of the responsibility to perform the services they are hired to give the public, and refrain from strikes while negotiations go on.

184

Sanitation Workers march in the Memphis Strike. The State brought in heavy artillery, as witnessed by the tank accompanying this marcher.

with Sanitation Workers there and establish for himself – and Local 831's rank and file – the exact nature of the link between Memphis and New York Sanitation Workers. In an interview, Nespoli explained: "It was at a meeting of the African-American Chapter of the department... this was after we had already negotiated the holiday as part of our contract... that I realized just how important it was to find out about the connection between our guys and the guys in Memphis."

Nespoli was accompanied by Business Agents Joe Middleton and Ronald Prattis. Greeted warmly by the AFSCME Local 1733, the union of Memphis Sanitation Workers, Nespoli and company spent an entire day interviewing veterans of the 1968 Memphis strike.

It was in Memphis that President Nespoli decided to hold the public ceremony that would properly commemorate the significance of the event. And

LOCAL 831 ARCHIVES

At left: This article from the leading newspaper in Memphis, The Scimitar, echoes Mayor Loeb's sentiment that Memphis wanted no part of the type of sanitation strike that New York City had just gone through and finished with two days earlier. Sanitation Workers in Memphis, however, did want part of it: the part that would give them higher wages and better working conditions.

ERNEST C. WITHERS, CHRYSLER MUSEUM OF ART

Sanitation Workers assemble en masse in a show of solidarity during the "I Am A Man Strke. Martin Luther King, Jr. was murdered while in Memphis to support the Strike.

so it was that seven weeks later, on January 17, 2008, the commemoration was held at Trinity Church. Harry Nespoli spoke first, speaking from his heart directly to his audience, without a written speech. He was the first to announce the union's connection of their 1968 strike with that of the "I Am A Man" strike in Memphis a week later. He explained: "What this Union was fighting for in 1968 was the same as the workers in Memphis – dignity and respect for the work they did."

Mayor Bloomberg also spoke, telling the Sanitation Workers gathered that "I have always been a big fan of you. Without you, we wouldn't have the quality of life that we do." The Mayor then spoke of Martin Luther King: "Although his life was cut tragically short, his words and deeds stand with us today. You are just as important in terms of taking what he said and making it a reality. The challenge never ends."

Jesse Epps, Martin Luther King's colleague, addressed the audience of five hundred strong, including more than three hundred shop stewards, and described the influence of the strike by New York Sanmen on their counterparts in Memphis:

It was you who gave them [Memphis Sanitation Workers] the courage to act. It was these men from New York, if I may use the colloquialism, that fired the shot and made America stand up and its conscience to be pricked and compelled Doctor King and others like him to come into the fray...

Epps said Memphis workers decided to walk the picket line after seeing

Harry Nespoli addresses a crowd of 500 Sanitation Workers and City officials at the first commemoration of Martin Luther King Day by Local 831.

how New York Sanitation Workers impacted the Big Apple with their own strike in February of 1968.

Holiday, Holy Day

The holiday meant different things to different members of the Union's rank and file. For some, it was another sign of respect from the City. For others, and certainly to the Union's brothers and sisters of color, the holiday had a personal significance.

Along the way to negotiating the holiday, a discovery was made that reinforced the importance of this event for every member of Local 831.

● ● ● ● ●

Harry Nespoli knows that the challenge never ends. "If Martin Luther King were alive today, he'd be fighting for those same Sanitation Workers in Memphis. Same here. The struggle begins again every day at the Union Hall."

But for this Local 831 president, it is a challenge that he looks forward to. "It's what keeps me going, it's what keeps the Union strong. Finding out about the connection between New York and Memphis, that's important. It's all part of our history, and it's a great history. It's all going into the book," says Nespoli, talking about the importance that he places on the writing of the Union's history. "The new guys coming on to the force, they need to know about this. They need to know what this Union has stood for, what it has fought for... for over 50 years."

Interviewed after the ceremony, veteran Sanitation Worker Willie Bryant said:

"For younger members in the department, this is an education. So I'm glad, not just because I'm black and he was black, but because we are brothers who all do the same job."

Chapter Sixteen

Rise and Shine

"It's nothing short of remarkable that there have been only four Union president over the 70 year history of 831. It says something about their leadership, about how important continuity... and building on past successes is to them."
   - Alan Klinger, labor lawyer and consultant to Local 831

Stand outside the headquarters of the Uniformed Sanitationmen's Association at 25 Cliff Street on any weekday morning about 5 a.m. and watch as business agents, Union executives and Union Stewards come to work. Their gait picks up as they approach the four-story brick building and many bound up the three steps, beating the doorman to the door. There is an athleticism to their movements. Even at rest, sitting or standing, the posture of a Sanitation Worker often appears poised for action.

And it starts with their boss, Harry Nespoli, who still moves something like a running back. Even diminutive John DeLury saw himself – and liked playing – cowboy and rodeo star, as he hog-tied city negotiators for forty years and – at age 63 – was still able to jump up onto the top of a panel truck in order to signal the start to the Strike of 1968... Jack Bigel, too, the perennial wrestler, always looked to take down any opponent who stood in the way of him – and Local 831 – coming out on top.

But their common trait is more than athleticism, more than the mere physical strength that one might naturally accord to a group of workers dubbed "New York's Strongest." What they share most is enthusiasm for their work and a commitment to each other. More than anything else, the Uniformed Sanitationmen's Association, Local 831 of the International Brotherhood of Teamsters, is about a bond between brothers – and sisters. The USA today is family.

Even Allen Brawer, consultant to Local 831, will address as "brother" or "sister" Sanitation Workers at stewards' meetings or negotiating committee meetings. Brawer carries on today in the tradition of Jack Bigel, in whose employ he worked for over twenty years. Although no wrestler, Brawer has shown dedication to Sanitation Workers over the long run, of which he knows something from the 17 New York marathons he has completed.

In 2009, more than 70 years after a small group of incinerator laborers formed the Uniformed Sanitationmen's Association, and just over a half-century since it became the exclusive representative of the city's Sanitationmen, there is still a spring in the step of this small but dynamic union.

It is a Union with a distinct identity – political, vocational and economic – and its rank-and-file hold their heads up high. Just as John DeLury served as Chair of the Public Employees Conference, so today Harry Nespoli chairs the Municipal Labor Committee, representing a wide cross-section of municipal employees.

Politically, Local 831 is once again becoming active on the local level from community boards to City Hall, as well as in the state and national arenas. In 2005 and 2006, the Cliff Street headquarters has hosted Senator Hillary Clinton and Mayor Michael Bloomberg. USA executives also visited former President Bill Clinton and presented him with a check for $10,000 – one for victims of the 2005 tsunami in Asia and a second for victims of Hurricane Katrina that same year. On any given day, the Union Hall plays revolving door to a raft of City Council members, assemblymen and other elected officials.

Vocationally, Sanitation Worker is one of the most sought-after jobs in the civil service today. Wages, benefits and the pension aside, the job has gained stature. Decades of stalwart service to the city has enhanced their image and the countless good deeds of Sanitation Workers, capped by their volunteer efforts in the cleanup after 9-11, have raised their public status. Former Deputy Mayor Randy Levine states it simply: "Sanitation Workers are heroes."

They are also considered smart. "They might not have college degrees," says Howard Rubenstein, "but they have street degrees. And I mean M.A.s and PhDs attached to them."

Long-gone are the days when Sanmen were disparaged as "garbage men." The term may still crop up here and there, but it has become almost archaic or simply isolated to the language of Sanitation Workers jibing each other. John DeLury, in a hundred different phrasings and on a thousand different occasions said "Don't call us garbage men. We may handle garbage, but it's not who we are." Anyway, it would have to be "garbage women" today, out of fairness to the 176 of women on the force. Or "garbage workers" or "garbage people," which sound either awkward or just plain comical. Not to mention the fact that a major part of the job, vocationally speaking, consists of snow removal. And no one is suggesting that Sanitation Workers be called snowmen, a calling if not job classification whose practitioners are more likely found, though not always working, at City Hall.

Executive Officers and Business Agents of Local 831 gather for a group photo in August 2009. The Brooklyn and Manhattan Bridges preside in the background. From left: Vincent Cassino, Director Retirees; Phil Servider, Business Agent; John Lewandowski, Business Agent; Jim Parker, Business Agent; Frank Assisi, Assist Admin Security Benefits; Jerry Merolla, Business Agent; Tom Bacigalupo, Trustee; Tony Lenza, Recording Secretary; Mike Bove, Secretary-Treasurer; Pasquale Amenta, Building Engineer; Harry Nespoli, President; Nick Pisano, Vice-President; Dennis Schock, Trustee; Tony Rodriguez, Trustee; Bill Corcoran, Business Agent; Mark Ostrowski, Admin Security Benefits; Steve Mignano, Business Agent; Ron Prattis, Business Agent; Nick Bauso, Business Agent; St. Joseph Middleton, Business Agent

Economically, Sanitation Workers have made it to the top of the heap. While other unions lingered over the issue of parity, the USA focused on productivity. As the Times pointed out in October 2005, the Sanitation Workers new contract at that time gave the USA "the largest raise won by any municipal union in the current round of bargaining."

The contract included what Mayor Michael Bloomberg hailed as an important productivity breakthrough: the one-man truck. USA president Harry Nespoli pointed out that the new one-man truck program would only apply to "containerized" large-bulk pickups and would start with just forty-five trucks. Nespoli also took the occasion to point out the $2.1 billion that the city had saved since the introduction of the two-man truck in 1980.

At the time of the contract's signing, Mayor Bloomberg praised Sanitation Workers for keeping the streets so clean, clearing the snow so promptly and starting work before dawn, under all kinds of weather conditions. Bloomberg

Shop Stewards enjoy a moment at a Stewards Meeting at the Cliff Street Union Hall.

said: "Outsiders at best do only what's asked. Insiders do what's needed. The challenge has been to find a way to give them [Sanitation Workers] the raises they deserve."

That was a challenge that the USA also welcomed. Harry Nespoli sums up: "In the end you have a better-paid force, more productivity and a better deal for the New York City taxpayer. And our guys, well, they can take care of their families. That's what it's all about, family."

The Future

The history as recorded in this book is over. But in many ways it never ends. Those who read this book will make their own history. What goes on is Local 831 and its membership:

- proud
- loyal
- unified
- determined
- hard working

And every day earning the DIGNITY AND RESPECT of the citizens of this great City.

Appendix A – Important Dates in the History of Local 831 IBT

Drivers and Hostlers Union (DHU) organize street cleaning workers **1882**

DHU strikes **1882, June 1907, 1911**

Creation of "White Wings" under SC Commissioner Waring; uniforms in use **1895 until 1935**

Labor Management Committee of 41 (one rep from each sanitation district) created to air grievances **1896**

Formation of Joint Council of Drivers and Sweepers **1918**

Sanitation workers represented by 21 different unions; four large unions of the Joint Council of Sweepers and Drivers emerge as the strongest **late1930s**

Establishment of the Association of Employees of Incinerators by John Joseph Conroy and John J. DeLury **1936**

DeLury becomes president of the AEI, Carmine Yorio VP, Harry Scharaga Financial Secretary" **1939**

AEI affiliates with the AFL and becomes Waste Disposal Local 61-44; changes name again to Association of Classified Employees of the Sanitation Department **1941**

ACESD becomes a member of the Joint Council **1941**

Sanitation Dept recognizes five unions of Joint Council as worker reps **May 1941**

Joint Council changes its name to Joint Council of Sanitation Locals; DeLury moves onto the Executive Board **1945**

Local 111-A of the Building Services Employees International AFSCME is charted and quickly becomes second largest sanitation union **1947**

ACESD affiliates with the International Brotherhood of Teamsters becoming Uniformed Sanitationmen's Association, Local 831 **1952**

Newly elected Mayor Robert F. Wagner publishes an "Interim Code for Collective Bargaining" as a guideline to municipal contract negotiations; Sanitation Workers are the first group to bargain and sign an agreement with the city **1954**

New York City transfers the responsibility for garbage pick-up from commercial establishments located in residential buildings to the private carters who already service stand alone businesses **1955**

USA overwhelmingly wins election against 111-A and receives a "Certificate of Exclusive Representation" to become the sole voice and bargaining agent for all New York City sanitation workers **Jan 27, 1956**

Wagner issues Executive Order 49 (the Little Wagner Act referring to the national law authored by the Mayor's father a generation before) giving city employees the right to join a labor union **1958**

Major unified work stoppage undertaken by members of Local 831 over pension and wage issues; they march three miles through Manhattan to City Hall and surround it while contract negotiations are in process **July 1960**

Local 831 evolves into an effective political machine flexing its new muscle in Mayor Wagner's third term election in 1961 **1960s**

Local 831 signs first ever collective bargaining agreement covering non-economic issues including specified grievance procedures; it is first NYC municipal union to have such a contract **Feb 8, 1961**

USA Record, newspaper of Local 831, begins publication **March 1965**

Taylor Law replaces Condon-Wadlin Act; creation of New York City Office of Collective Bargaining and the Office of Municipal Labor Relations; makes strikes by city workers illegal and provides for steep penalties. **1966**

USA nine day strike; DeLury goes to jail for leading the strike **February 1968**

Arbitration panels awards sanitation workers 90% wage parity to other uniformed city workers such as police officers and firefighters **1971**

John DeLury becomes spokesman for the coalition of all New York state and municipal workers in their fight to protect pensions from the cutbacks proposed by the State Pension Commission headed by Otto Kinzel **1973**

Wildcat three day strike by USA members led by Harry Nespoli in reaction 2,934 layoff notices forced by the NYC fiscal crisis **July 1975**

Local 831 first union to sign a contract with New York City to include a clause covering sharing of the savings produced by increased productivity **1977**

Eddie Ostrowski becomes the second president of the USA as John DeLury retires **1978**

John DeLury dies **1980**

Work to contract action protesting possible layoffs **Nov 1990**

Pete Scarlatos becomes the third president of the USA as Eddie Ostrowski retires **1993**

Harry Nespoli becomes the fourth president of the USA as Pete Scarlatos retires **2002**

Martin Luther King, Jr. holiday for Local 831 members **2008**

Appendix B – Chronology of Local 831 Working Conditions and Benefit Improvements

---

Equality of Work and Pay
  Elimination of Driver and Loader titles, creation of new title,
  Sanitationman with one pay rate 1956

Work Week
  48 hour work week (reduced from 60+) 1936
  44 hour work week 1952
  42 hour work week 1953
  40 hour work week .... July 1, 1956

Collective Bargaining
  First Collective Bargaining Agreement including
  specified grievance procedures .... Feb 8, 1961

Overtime
  Time and one-half for Saturday work after six hours ...... Oct 1, 1968
  Double time for Sunday 1968

Night Shift Differential
  Paid for any work shift with four or more hours falling after 3pm 1965

Productivity
Gainsharing From Two-Worker Truck Program
  Implementation of two-worker per collection truck and the
  division of the savings between the employer and
  the employees; workers receive savings in the form
  of a truck differential per worked shift .... May 1, 1982

Productivity
Gainsharing From One-Worker Truck Program
  Implementation of one-worker "Roll-on/Roll-off" truck and the
  division of the savings between the employer and
  the employees; workers receive savings in the form of a
  truck differential per worked shift .... Jan 9, 2006

Productivity
Gainsharing From Route Extension Program
Implementation of route extensions and the division of the
the savings between the employer and the employees; workers
receive savings in the form of a differential per each shift
attaining the performance targets   March 3, 2000

Productivity
Gainsharing From "Dumping-on-Shift" Program
Implementation of "Dumping-on-Shift" and the division of the
the savings between the employer and the employees; workers
receive savings in the form of a differential per each shift
attaining the performance targets   Jan 9, 2006

Longevity Payment
Payment after five years of service   July 1, 1984
Expansion of longevity payment schedule to include
payments after ten, fifteen, and twenty years of service   July 1, 1990

Uniform Allowance
Employer payment for cleaning and maintenance of
the required uniform   1954
First increase followed by subsequent raises   1956

Health Insurance
Employer assumption of 100% of premium costs for all
active sanitation workers and dependents   Jan 1, 1966
Employer assumption of 100% of premium costs for all
sanitation workers who retired from January 1, 1965   Jan 1, 1966

Security Benefits Fund
Creation of Security Benefits Fund for all active
Sanitationmen to provide benefits supplemental to
those offered by the citywide health plan;
Fund began operations on November 19, 1962.   Jan 1, 1962

Retirees Security Benefits Fund
Creation of Security Benefits Fund for all retired
Sanitationmen to provide benefits supplemental to
those offered by the citywide health plan   Jan 1, 1975

Compensation Accrual Fund
Base Employer Contribution
Creation of Compensation Accrual Fund providing
supplemental income for retirement   April 1, 1967

Compensation Accrual Fund
Employer Contribution for Employees Working on Shifts
Meeting Agreed to Refuse and Recycling Targets:
Productivity Savings Program (PSP)

Creation of an additional employer contribution to the
Compensation Accrual Fund   Jan 9, 2006

Compensation Accrual Fund
Employer Contribution for Employees with 15 Years
or More of Service

Creation of an additional employer contribution to the
Compensation Accrual Fund   April 2, 2008

Retiree Supplemental Annuity Fund

Creation of a new fund for all sanitation workers with
a normal service retirement of at least twenty years;   July 1, 2009

Retirement Provisions

Years of service needed to retire: 30   1929
Age 55 eligibility
Social Security coverage   1957
Years of service needed to retire: 25   April 1963
Elimination of age 55 eligibility; reduced pension
Employer contribution of 75%, employee 25%
Years of service needed to retire: 25   1964
Pension equal to ½ of final year's compensation
Beginning of ITHP – employer assumes first 2.5% of   Dec 10, 1965
employee's pension contribution
Years of service needed to retire: 20
Pension equal to ½ of final year's compensation   July 3, 1967
Tier II   July 1, 1973
Years of service needed to retire: 25
Final compensation equal to any three years of salary
Tier IV   July 1, 1983
Mandatory employee pension contribution of 3%
Tier II modified   July 1, 1992
Years of service needed to retire: 20
Mandatory employee pension contribution
Final compensation equal to any three years of salary
Tier II modified   July 1, 2000
Employee contributions for the first ten years only
Heart Bill   July 1, 2005
Three-quarter disability for those sanitation workers
retiring with heart disease

Appendix C – Summary of History Regarding Pensions

Provision for financial security in a sanitation worker's post-employment years has always been a critical issue for sanitation workers. While wages and conditions of employment are defined by contract, pension benefits are set by State legislation. The attainment of each of the benefits was usually the culmination of log practices. Given the cost associated with a pension benefit the City has traditionally fought improvements and sought to reduce its cost.

The initial full pension benefit of the Relief and Pension Fund of the Department of Street Cleaning was a minimum of one-half pay after 25 years of service. Sanitation employees were considered non-uniformed city employees. Compared to the pensions received at the time by most other non-uniformed city workers, this was a generous benefit. Financing the retirement benefit was a mandatory employee contribution equal to 3% of wages supplemented by annual employer contributions covering the cost of the current year benefit payout and administrative costs. This pension was funded on a pay as you go basis rather than actuarially as are modern retirement systems.

Though initially most DoSC retirees were not eligible for a full pension, the benefit would be decreased 16 years later as more and more DoSC employees began working long enough to collect a full pension based on their years of service. Requirements for a full retirement benefit for sanitation workers would not again equal those enacted in 1913 and eliminated in 1929 until 1964.

Beginning operations in October, 1911, the Relief and Pension Fund started granting pensions on January 1, 1913. In its second year, the average age of retirement was about 59-60 with 16 years of service. At the end of the 1920s, the average retirement age hadn't changed appreciably but the years of service had increased to 22 or 23.

The rate of street sweepers and drivers killed on the job in 1914, 10 per 10,000 workers, was higher that year than the job related death rate for police officers, 7 per 10,000. In 1914, five sweepers and two drivers died while working for the Department of Street Cleaning and 938 men were seriously injured. The years of work in these conditions quickly took its toll. Of the 73 sweepers retiring in 1914, more than ten percent (8) died within one year.

On December 1, 1929 the New York City Department of Sanitation was established by merging the city's Department of Street Cleaning with the street cleaning bureaus of Queens and Richmond counties. Simultaneously with the creation of the city's Sanitation Department, the Relief and Pension Fund was closed to new participants. All future employees of the new citywide agency were made eligible to join the larger and actuarially based New York City Employees Retirement System.

This retirement system for all city employees other than police, fire, and teachers had been proposed by a mayoral commission originally appointed in 1913 to study the retirement needs of the city's employees. NYCERS was created by an amendment to the city's charter passed by the state legislature in 1920. Though pensions are locally funded and administered, all laws affecting New York City municipal retirement systems must be enacted by the state: approved by the Assembly and the Senate and signed by the Governor.

NYCERS was run by a Board of Trustees composed of the members of the city's old Board of Estimate and Apportionment: the Mayor, Comptroller, City Council President, and the five Borough Presidents. At its start there were no employee representatives among the Trustees. The city's Comptroller was the custodian of NYCERS funds. Investments were only permitted in municipal or other governmental bonds. Initially, NYCERS effectively became a bank for the City of New York: the city would put money in as its pension contribution and then take it back in the form of a loan (i.e., general obligation bond). It wasn't until 1953 that the Comptroller received legal permission to invest some of NYCERS' funds in common stocks with the possibility of higher returns (and risks).

NYCERS accepted its first participants in October of 1920. Upon joining, sanitation members were assigned to one of three employment categories based on the extent of physical and mental exertion needed to complete a job. Each grouping was further subdivided by gender. When employees of the new DoS were incorporated into the system, sweepers or loaders were categorized as "laborers" and drivers, known at the time as chauffeurs, were considered "skilled" or "mechanics."

These categorizations were not innocent of consequences. Though the differences were not great, each of the three had unique minimum retirement ages and service requirements defining eligibility for a full pension. Different life spans were assumed for each group because of the nature of the work performed and so each had their own actuarial (tables that are used to measure the probability of a worker with a cerain age and seervcie) living to a certain age.

Service requirements for a full pension in NYCERS were more stringent than those needed to receive a benefit from the old Relief and Pension Fund of the Department of Street Cleaning. As the Depression approached, newly hired Department of Sanitation employees would have to work longer to collect a full pension than their fathers. Street sweepers or loaders in Group

I (laborers) needed to be 58 years of age and have had 33 years of service to be eligible for a full pension. Drivers in Group II (skilled workers or mechanics) needed an additional year of age and service (59 and 34) to retire with an undiminished pension.

The full retirement benefit provided these Department of Sanitation employees now NYCERS members was equal to one-half of an individual's "final salary" which was initially defined as the average of his last ten years of work. It was funded by both the city's contribution ("pension") and the employee's contribution ("annuity") and the interest earned on both. The original intention of NYCERS' creators was that the benefit would be funded equally by the employer and the employee.

Depending on gender, age at hire and into what group a title was assigned, employee contributions to NYCERS varied. For example at age 20, they ranged from 3.86% of salary (male mechanics) downward to 1.44% (female clerks).

When those Sanitation workers hired in the 1930s and 1940s began to retire, the portion of their final full retirement benefit funded by their own contributions amounted to somewhat less than 40%. Their annual contributions were based on the low wages they received most of their working lifetimes.

Immediately upon joining, NYCERS offered sanitation workers a job related disability benefit. They were eligible for an ordinary disability benefit after ten years of service.

Any modifications of retirement plans might originate with the Municipal Assembly (equivalent to today's City Council) but could only be enacted into law by the state's legislature. This process for pension change was confirmed in 1925. Two years later the first of a series of alterations and expansions of the benefits available through NYCERS was passed by the legislature. The definition of final average salary was changed to the average of the last five years of work. Ten years later in 1937 it was further altered to the average of an employee's five best consecutive years of work.

In the year before sanitation workers became eligible to join NYCERS, the system created an optional pension at a lower retirement age, 55, and service requirement, 30 years. To receive this pension, an employee would have to declare so at entry because he would have to pay into the system a higher contribution (from 4.52% for laborers to 5.03% for clerks).

Loans were first offered to NYCERS members the year after sanitation workers became eligible. Beginning in 1930, they were able to borrow up to 25% of that portion of their account for which they contributed. In 1938 this percentage was increased to 40%, to 50% in 1957, and eventually to 75%.

Though not tied directly to NYCERS, sanitation workers' retirement package was greatly enhanced in 1957 with the addition of Social Security. When it was created in the 1930s, the federal Social Security program excluded local and state governments. Congress in 1954 changed this provision by giving these employers the option of joining.

Meeting in extraordinary session in the spring of 1957, the Assembly and Senate of New York state enacted legislation permitting the state's public employers to offer Social Security coverage. On June 27 of 1957, the city's Board of Estimate passed a local law enabling members of NYCERS to join Social Security. It also gave city employees the option to offset their NYCERS contribution by the amount they were paying into Social Security.

The most profound changes to the pensions available to sanitation workers came in the decade of the 1960s after the formation of a strong and united Local 831 with the rights of collective bargaining. The union created a forceful presence at the City Council and in Albany. It clearly communicated to the public the nature of the job and the toll it extracted on workers. Because of this, changes came steadily throughout the decade.

In May of 1960, the City began to assume the first 2.5% of its employees' NYCERS contributions. This became known as ITHP (Increased Take Home Pay). In 1965, the contribution split between the city and the sanitation worker which had been 50/50 since 1929 was modified to 75/25.

Sanitation workers won retirement after 25 years of service with no age requirement in 1963. But the benefit was a reduced (36% of final average salary) pension. The next year legislation passed providing for a half-pay benefit. It was equal to the full retirement allowance of the old Relief and Pension Fund of the Department of Street Cleaning eliminated with the termination of the Fund in 1929. It took sanitation workers 35 years to gain back something that had been lost in their grandfathers' generation. The next step would be to best it.

Three years later during collective bargaining negotiations, Local 831 got the city to agree to support a 20 year retirement bill. Introduced in February of 1967, it was unanimously passed by the legislature and on April 10 Governor Nelson Rockefeller with John DeLury at his side signed it into law. It provided sanitation workers with a pension equal to one-half final salary at 20 years of service with no age requirement. It went into effect in July. After many years of hard political work, Local 831 had achieved a pension equal to those offered the other members of New York City's uniformed services.

In addition to the 20 year service retirement, by the end of the 1960s sanitation workers were also eligible for a three-quarter of final salary accidental disability pension and an ordinary disability pension either at one-third pay (with up to ten years of service) or half pay (with at least ten years of service).

The 20 year service retirement covering all sanitation workers lasted a little more than six years. It was killed by a growing anti-public employee clamor in the guise of "pension reform." The Uniformed Sanitation Workers and its then president John J. Delury led the fight to protect the retirement benefits of municipal and state workers. DeLury became chairman of the New York State Conference of Public Employee Organizations and held that position through-out the early 1970s.

But all the concentrated efforts of the Conference and DeLury and the other union leaders couldn't counter the immense pressure exerted by the Governor and his NYS Permanent Commission on Public Employee Pension and Retirement Systems. The Commission issued a report in 1972 that indelibly framed the discussion around "ballooning costs" and "exorbitant benefits." The Governor called the legislature into extraordinary session and it established a new retirement structure for NYCERS and the other public systems in the state. Its reduced pension provisions became known as "Tier II."

Replacing the 20 year pension was a new "Tier II" benefit. Sanitation workers hired from July 1, 1973 were eligible to retire with a full pension after 25 years of service. Final average salary was defined as the average of any three consecutive years of work; if in any one year the salary was more than 20% higher than the salaries in the other two years, the amount of compensation above the 20% limit was excluded for purposes of pension calculating. The 1973 legislation also made pensions a non-negotiable item between public employees and their employers during collective bargaining.

Beginning with Tier IV in 1983, all sanitation workers along with other NYCERS members were required to contribute 3% of their annual salary towards their pensions as long as they were working. Previously employee contributions varied by age and date of hire.

As in the years 1929 through 1964, the work of Local 831 since 1973 has been to win back for newly hired sanitation workers the retirement benefits enjoyed by those hired before the creation of Tier II. The union has to date been successful in regaining most of what had been lost.

In 1992, the Tier II retirement benefit in effect for almost two decades was modified. Newly hired sanitation workers would again have a full pension after 20 years of service without any age requirement but unlike in the 1960s, they were required to contribute at a higher rate and their final salary continued to be defined as a three year average, not the annual rate on their last day of work as in Tier I. Incumbents could also elect the new 20 year pension by buying into the new program. In 2000, the required basic contribution of 3% was limited to the first ten years of service.

Tier IV sanitation workers in 2002 won a three-quarter of salary accidental disability pension. In 2003 Local 831 lobbied strongly in Albany for a bill providing a three quarter disability pension for all those sanitation workers with heart disease. This would put them on par with other uniformed services. The assumption behind the bill is that the disease was connected to the nature of the work. The City then has the obligation to prove otherwise or the pension was granted. The legislature enacted the law in 2004 and it went into effect on July 1, 2005.

Almost from the beginning of public employee pensions, the need for some mechanism to protect retirees from the erosion of their benefits through inflation was evident. Of course, it was most felt in periods of greater price hikes such as the 1970s and the early 1990s. At times, sanitation workers did receive a one-time cost-of-living-adjustment but clearly it wasn't sufficient.

Not until 1995 was legislation passed that provided an automatic on-going "COLA" to retirees.

Recently a major addition was added to post employment benefits. The Retiree Supplemental Annuity Fund was established in 2009. Each year the Trustees will determine the extent that a supplemental payment can be made to those who retired with a full service retirement benefit. The funding for the program is collectively bargained with the City.

A significant difference from somewhat similar benefits that other uniformed forces have is that this benefit can also be paid to those who retired before the date of establishment of the benefit.

Sources and References

The majority of the information gathered in this book owes to research performed in the Microforms Room 100 of the New York Public Library at Fifth Avenue and 42nd Street.

There I gained access to newspapers going back to the mid-1800s. The New York Times, in particular, provided detailed, although often biased against unions, material. Further research was done in the Archives Room of the Civil Service newspaper, The Chief. The archives of Local 831, consisting of thirty years of union publications, was immeasurably helpful.

Interviews with the following individuals were also most helpful:

- NYC Mayor Michael Bloomberg
- Justice Robert Sweet
- Former DC 37 Executive Director Victor Gotbaum
- Public Relations Consultant Howard Rubenstein
- Former NYC Deputy Mayor Randy Levine
- Former Local 831 Presidents Edward Ostrowski and Peter Scarlatos
- Department of Sanitation Commissioner John Doherty
- Management Consultant and former Chair of the Tri-Partite Panel, Robert Schrank
- Former Chair of the Tri-Partite Panel Alton Marshall
- DSNY First Deputy Commissioner Michael Bimonte
- Allen Brawer
- Former Local 237 President Barry Feinstein
- Former Sanitation Commissioner Norman Steisel
- dozens of NYC Sanitation Workers
- numerous others

Name Index

Subject Index